Out West

Out West

Stories About
Persons and Places
on the Canadian Prairies

Bob Phillips

Western Producer Prairie Books
Saskatoon, Saskatchewan

Cover design by Wm. Perehudoff
Photos by GIBSON PHOTOS LTD.

Printed and bound in Canada by MODERN PRESS
⬅️➡️ l
Saskatoon, Saskatchewan

Western Producer Prairie Books publications are produced and manufactured in the middle of western Canada by a unique publishing venture owned by a group of prairie farmers who are members of Saskatchewan Wheat Pool. Our first book in 1954 was a reprint of a serial originally carried in *The Western Producer*, a weekly newspaper providing news and information to western farm families since 1923. We continue the tradition of providing enjoyable and informative reading for all Canadians.

Canadian Cataloguing in Publication Data

Phillips, Bob, 1921-
    Out west

    Includes index.
    ISBN 0-919306-93-4

    1. Prairie Provinces. 2. Prairie
Provinces — Biography. I. Title.
FC3231.P54 971.2 C77-002208-1
F1060.9

Contents

Relations

Why This Book?

This little book was prepared by a newspaperman from reports on his ramblings across western Canada during more than twenty-five years. It is not a catalogue of western persons and places, nor is it a social history. It is a collection of short pieces written to meet newspaper deadlines, by a westerner who has lived elsewhere and realizes that some things are different out here. Some writers have described the West as a place with little past but plenty of future. Farmers especially often speak of it being "next year country." Most of the settlers came with an expectation that the place held a future for them, and that kind of hope persists and permeates every facet of life.

Settlement is not yet 100 years old. Native Indians roamed this country for centuries, and explorers and fur traders went through it 300 years ago. But the first railway track did not reach Regina, in the very center of the plains until 1883, and it took another generation before settlement was general. The railway made migration possible, but it was the revolution in wheat production which brought the immigrants. Men and women from other continents flooded into what early geographers had called a semi-arid desert unfit for habitation. What changed the situation was man's ability to adapt. A new hardy variety of wheat was developed to withstand the short growing season, and summerfallow was practised to conserve the limited soil moisture. While this was happening on the prairies, world wheat prices rose because of increased demand, at the same time as oceanic freight rates declined. The West this little book talks about is the West that grew out of the wheat.

In time there were many changes. Ever better varieties of wheat were bred with improved yield and quality and resistance to the many blights which come to infest the crop. Marketing techniques and institutions were developed to meet the new environment. Out of these changes came both the farmer co-operatives and, later, the central marketing agency called the Canadian Wheat Board. Tractors replaced the horses, and gasoline the oats and fodder allowing expansion in the size of farm an individual could husband. Other kinds of changes have followed.

There are idealists out west, of course, but the over-riding philosophy is pragmatism, the notion that the facts of history should be read for their practical lessons. Analysts from elsewhere are always trying to find the reason for the innovations introduced out west, and some of them will not accept the simple explanation that we do what we do because it works. Early settlers built sod houses because sod was all there was; they became co-operatively minded because each family needed the help of its neighbors to raise a barn roof or fight a prairie fire.

This selection of articles attempts to provide a representative sampling of some of the changes which have occurred and continue to occur; it introduces some of the persons and places unique to western Canada; and it contains a few items about the author's family which he suggests is representative of many others who have made the West. The men and women whose life and times are discussed in this little book have each helped to make the West a better place for all of us. Without them, much would have been impossible, including this book.

Acknowledgments

The following persons deserve special thanks for their contributions:

- The persons and places about whom these stories are written.
- Jean Bolton and Joyce Ozeroff who typed the manuscripts.
- Murray Gibson whose fine photographs appear throughout.
- The men and women of Western Producer Publications whose crafts and trades brought this book through all its production stages.

Despite all of this help, the author remains responsible for all errors of commission or omission.

Change

Life is Changing Out West

The Canadian prairies are changing. People across the West live a different way of life than they did back in the 1940s and 1950s, a generation and more ago. The way they do their jobs is changing; sometimes even their faces look changed. It has not, of course, happened overnight. Many who live here scarcely realize how different things now are.

Take roads. Prairie roads were once the brunt of every passing motorist's jest. They were narrow, rough, muddy in season, and almost always bad. Now the prairie has straight, wide, hard-topped ribbons of pavement. Main highways are as good as any on the continent, and secondary roads are fast becoming excellent.

This change in the roads has done as much as anything to change the life of the man who lives on the prairie. The farmer now may get more easily to town; he often lives there and commutes daily in seeding and harvest time to his land. His trucks move faster, and he needs fewer men to help him haul his grain. He can move heavy farm equipment, now properly rubber-tired, along these roads from field to field and consequently can work his land more easily. That also takes fewer hired hands.

Regina is the heart of the prairie. It houses the world's largest grain marketing co-operative, and grain is still the lifeblood of the prairie. The city was built when the prairies were entered, and its growth has paralleled the progress of the land which surrounds it. Its business life ebbs and flows with the prosperity of the farmer and the weather, soil conditions, rainfall, heat, rust, insects, weeds;

hail and frost — the farmers' ever-present worries — are still the main conversation pieces. During the winter, grain is still a sure-fire topic: boxcar movements, delivery quotas, grain sales and prices, and, of course, next year's prospects.

Around Regina the change is as great as anywhere on the prairie. Farmers who not so many years ago tilled prairie grassland with horses and a plowshare now farm two or more whole sections of wheat land with expensive, high-powered machinery. This change to more mechanized wheat farming has contributed greatly to the changed face of the prairie. Expanding acreage has left deserted small farmsteads, useful only as storage space for grain the farmer cannot readily market. In the move to bigger landholding, small schools and churches have also been left deserted. Farmers drive past the village store and shop in the nearby town or city. Their children go to school in town. The family goes to the town church.

Farmers no longer depend on one crop. Where once they grew only wheat, they now seed feed grains, the new oilseeds and even specialty crops like field peas and sunflowers. In areas of all three prairie provinces, irrigation has been introduced. Besides, more farmers have added livestock to their farming enterprises all across the prairies.

There is more than a revolution in wheat farming to change the prairie scene. Oil, discovered on wheat land in all three prairie provinces, has brought new industry, and more is expected. And there is potash in Saskatchewan. The prairie already has some secondary industries: coal is mined, table salt and fertilizers are produced, iron pipe processed, and industrial machinery assembled. Many other ventures are investigating the market and its power-from-oil potential.

Horses have been displaced by machinery and trucks. A few years ago, horsemen around Swift Current organized a horse-meat co-operative to process food and feed for the rest of Canada and abroad. The plant long since closed when there were no more prairie horses to process.

These changes have helped give prairie people an easier life in a country of harsh elements; they have given them more net income and greater leisure. The influx of other industry is stabilizing the prairie economy, hedging the farmer's community against the sharp, cruel void of a crop failure. In their wake, however, have gone some of the things that made life just a little different on the prairie back, say, thirty or forty years ago. Some of these things still cling heavily to memory.

Grain no longer stands in stooks to dry and ripen before being forked on to a rack and hauled to the thresher. It now lies in long flat swaths which eventually are scooped up mechanically by a combine harvester. Freight-train locomotives no longer wail in the night and spin smoke trails as they move across the prairie with their long line of boxcars. Modern diesels now pull trains, and they make no smoke. Their whistle doesn't wail; it squeals and screeches. Coal-oil lamps don't twinkle in farmhouse windows, and farmers don't swing lanterns as they trudge to their milking in the early hours. Most farms now have electric power. And most farmers buy their milk from the city dairy. The dusty smell of wheat at harvest time seems different. Often the same wisp of wind brings along some diesel fumes from a farm tractor, a passing truck, or even the pungent smell from crude oil being pumped.

And the hotels and eating places have changed. Custom has moved out to the highway — often bypassing the village completely — where modern motels and drive-in cafés have taken over. It's different all right from the days of the old porcelain basin and the pitcher of water that used to greet the prairie traveller's morning.

The Meadow Lark Still Sings in Springtime

The meadow lark sings in springtime. Spring is my favorite season. People who write dictionaries describe spring as the season when vegetation begins, but it is much more than that to me and, I suspect, to most of us. It is the season when the birds return, when animals arise from hibernation, when foliage returns to the trees and flowers to the fields. To the farmer it is the season for planting and seeding and for the renewal of hope for a crop to come.

The other day I drove across half a province to a series of farmers' meetings, thoroughly enjoying the trip because it provided the opportunity to renew acquaintance with the sights and sounds of spring on the prairies. It also gave me a chance, seldom available in these days of hustle and bustle, to think back on earlier times when I had enjoyed spring in other places.

One of my earliest recollections was of my boyhood on the prairies when I used to take the annual Easter holiday from school on an uncle's farm near Boharm, Saskatchewan. It was there I learned first about the call of the meadow lark and watched keen eyed for the first adventuresome gopher to poke his head up from his winter's hole along the roadside. It was there I learned to mimic the call of the lark, which I still remember sounds something like "I was here a year ago." The meadow lark still calls in exactly the same way from the prairie fence post in April.

Farmers everywhere along the route were out this year kicking at the damp soil and wondering aloud when the fields might be dry enough to take the first seeding. Some had found conditions suitable and had already made their first turns of the field.

I recalled another spring in the wilderness of the northern bush when I had hurried with others to pull stakes of a winter survey camp. The rush was to cross the frozen lakes with the cat train — and get beyond to civilization before the icy roadway melted in the spring breakup. Axes rang the louder that year in the clear spring air, the chatter of the jay was shriller, and the sunrise more brilliant each day than it had been the day before.

One spring in wartime I had watched the snow melt under the rain that drove over the wooded flats of an army camp near Debert in Nova Scotia. As the color slowly returned that year to the land and the hills beyond, we had been moved to the rolling valley of the St. John River, to regroup for a trip overseas, they had said. That year spring came in much the same way another must have for the poet Bliss Carman who had written:

> She comes with gusts of laughter,
> The music as of rills;
> With tenderness and sweetness,
> The wisdom of the hills.

Another spring had found me in the Canadian mountains as ice and snow began receding from their rocky peaks. Then, tiny streams gained momentum as they raced down from the top, becoming torrents of runoff as they reached the valleys below. They washed across and through roadways that year, tearing out bridges, and flooding rail and communication lines in one of the worst floods in British Columbia history. That was a spring with a roar.

But beyond the last coastal range all was quiet and peaceful along the roadsides of Vancouver Island where the daffodils waved in the soft breeze, and the old ladies mended the rose trellises leading to their cottages. I was back to the island again this year, and the daffodils waved again, and I was told the roses on the trellises were out.

Once I met the Canadian spring from aboard an ocean

liner as it steamed up the St. Lawrence River, home-bound
from Europe. Along the river, the trees and the flowers
were just coming to life. The snow along the north bank
still clung as if defying as long as possible the warm sun
which already had turned the south side into a quiet carpet
of new spring flowers and grass.

I've welcomed the Canadian spring from many vantage
points across this vast country, but spring on the prairies
remains my favorite. I suspect it is the contrast which
makes it so. Only a few weeks ago much of the prairie was
wind-swept and snowbound with little color other than
white and grey and only the sound of the wind to break the
stillness. But melting snow revealed first the dark greys
and black of the grain lands and then the yellow and silver
of last year's grassland. Already the grass is turning green,
the wild flowers are coming back to life, and a variety of
sounds have been added. The whine of the winter wind
has gone and in its place is a babble of new sounds: the
hum of machinery being started up for the first time this
year, the occasional bleat of a spring lamb and the more
frequent bawling of many new calves, dogs barking with
renewed enthusiasm, and the shout of human voices. But
above them all is the shrill song of the meadow lark,
repeating over and over again:

"I was here a year ago, I was here a year ago, I was
here a year ago."

Harvest Time

The Canadian West dons a colorful cloak and a mood of quiet thanksgiving when the harvest work is done in the fall. Along the route from the plains of Manitoba to the shore of British Columbia, the traveller sees an array of color. There are the yellows, browns, and sunset reds of the prairie grain fields and the soft blue of autumn skies. There are the dull greys and the lacy purples of the foothills, and the sharp white and black of the early snows on the peaks of the Rockies. There are the bright greens and the ripe reds and yellows in the orchards along the valleys that nestle among the British Columbia ranges. Finally there is the sea, the sparkling blue of the Pacific.

These are the colors that come every year to the western plains and foothills and mountains. To those who live out here, they are the welcome blanket that falls slowly after a summer of seeding and tilling and pruning in the grain fields and garden patches, in the orchards and the vineyards. They signal the relaxing end of the harvest, the farmers' rest before the long winter.

A trip through the Canadian West in all the warmth and splendor of any harvest season is a special delight. My route went from west to east, winding its way among Chilliwack, Princeton, and Cranbrook in British Columbia; Pincher Creek, Lethbridge, and Medicine Hat in Alberta; Swift Current, Regina, and Indian Head in Saskatchewan; Virden and then Brandon in Manitoba. Everywhere there were signs of a harvest hustle and bustle. There were also signs in the lowlands of heavy frost and in the mountains of early snow. The harvest could not last much longer.

In British Columbia, harvest colors were bright: the apples and the peaches were red, the plums full and purplish blue, the pears yellow. The grass was a greener green, revived by the early fall rains. By each orchard gate, small and large wooden crates climbed in mountainous stacks, awaiting the trucks that would take the bulk of the crop away to cannery or to the housewife's market. In Alberta there was the sugar-beet harvest. Farmers dug the root by machine and hand; trucks and wagons hauled it to the railway line where it was stacked awaiting movement to the sugar factory.

There was also grain; across the flat expanse of Saskatchewan and Manitoba there was mostly grain. There were some old-fashioned stooks and an occasional threshing machine spewing the rich bread wheat out one spout and straw out another. But mostly there were modern combines. Everywhere there were trucks and wagons. They hauled grain from one field to another where farmer-owned granaries would store it until elevator space could be found. Across the prairies, over the foothills, and through the mountains, freight trains seemed longer than at any other time.

In some districts farmers had good cause to rejoice. In others they had not. Some said there had been too little rain; some said too much at the wrong time; some cursed insects, rust, hail, wind, and early frosts, all of which had contributed to the annual gnawing-away of the yield. In some districts there was not enough left to bother about.

Everywhere it was colorful in the West, and the farmers' fight with nature was slowing into a lazy, relaxed autumn. It was a time for thanksgiving all along the road from the wind-swept fields of Manitoba to the Pacific. The harvest was all but in.

A Winter to Remember

Most people have a winter to remember. Mine was the winter of 1940-41, the winter I spent in the bush in northern Saskatchewan with a survey party under the direction of the late Fred Lamb of Saskatoon. The whole experience was new and strange for a city boy who was only nineteen. It was the first time I'd ever seen tall timber or been in the bush, the first time I'd seen and ridden on a cat train and a dog sled, the first time I'd used snowshoes, and certainly the first time I'd lived under canvas in temperatures which dipped on occasion to sixty degrees below zero Fahrenheit.

The other day I found a notebook kept that winter and some of the notations make interesting reading, many years later.

January 2: "I finally got away from Big River with three men and about 2,700 pounds of supplies on the cat train operated by Big River Fisheries. Fred Lamb was to wait for further supplies and would join us with the others by a second cat train a few days later. We got to Jack Rae's stopping place on Stoney Lake about seven P.M. and after supper set out across the lake going due north."

The cat train was powered with a crawler tractor up front and had three sleighs and a caboose, slung one after the other but several yards apart to prevent them all going into the water if the ice happened to break. There was a crew of four, two men on the job at once and two sleeping in the caboose. And it was so cold that one man could only spend a few minutes at a time on the unprotected seat of the cat. It made a regular run into the bush, taking in supplies for the fish camps and bringing out frozen fish. Our survey party was extra baggage that night.

January 6: "We were off by eight P.M. for our first day on the line. I shall never forget today, it nearly killed me. I'd never been on snowshoes before and it got me in the legs along with a few other places."

January 28: "This morning we saw a pack of timber wolves nearby, and they scared all our boys nearly out of their skins."

There were nine of us: the engineer with me as instrument man, a cook and a bull cook, four axemen and a chainman. Our job was to cut a skyline through the timber and measure the distance for the boundary of a game preserve which started on the northwest corner of Prince Albert National Park and ran twenty-four miles north and west.

January 30: "Trouble developed tonight. The men pushed for increased wages and threatened to walk out of the bush. At present they are getting a dollar fifty a day plus living."

February 26: "I broke the last mantle of the lamp tonight and was resigned to using candles for the rest of the winter. But two new mantles turned up in Shorty's pocket."

March 6: "Spent all day cutting a new trail to a new campsite. Two men were careless, and the horses ate their sandwiches."

March 31: "Today we finished work on the line, recutting the base line to NE 34-60-7-3 about five and a half miles east of our camp on Caribou Lake. Tomorrow we break camp and head for Big River and civilization."

Downhill Skiing

There's nothing quite like skiing down a steep mountain-side. Once you've pointed the ski tips downward and taken off you're committed on one of the most exciting rides possible. The point of no return occurs very early in a ski run because it's impossible to ski back up again on most mountainsides, and there's simply no other way down. Besides, while you're on the ride down it's almost impossible to keep anything else on your mind except survival. If you lose control you could have a nasty, even crippling tumble.

There is some evidence that people have been skiing for about 4,500 years. I've learned, for example, that a ski was found in a bog at Hoting in Sweden which is believed to be 4,500 years old. The pictorial representation of skiing has also been found on a rock near Rodoy in northern Norway dating back to about 2,000 B.C. Skis were used by Vikings during their raids on Norway in the tenth and eleventh centuries.

But sport skiing probably dates back only about 100 years or so, to the 1860s when the first secure bindings were invented by a Norwegian. Earlier skis were attached to the boot only at the toe, and the Norwegian invention secured the boot to the ski, allowing the skier to make turns and jumps. In more recent years secure bindings have been developed even further, and now one of the main objectives is to find a binding which will detach itself at the proper time during a fall to help the skiers avoid broken bones but will keep itself secure otherwise. The more sophisticated the binding and the release mechanism, the more costly the binding.

Some prairie settlers brought skis when they came west and others made their own because they soon found skis a welcome vehicle in the deep snow of the cold winters. But sport skiing has come more recently to the West and is much more vigorous than the skiing which pioneers knew.

For example, let me give you some idea of the rigors of the ski slopes in the Banff area of western Canada. Ski runs are measured in two ways: length of the run and vertical rise. The longest and fastest run in the Banff area is the North American run at Norquay which is reported to be 8,248 feet down a drop of 2,450 feet. The longest, steepest run at Lake Louise is down a vertical drop of 2,101 feet, while Sunshine provides a run with a vertical drop of 1,820 feet. It is possible to pick and choose the run, even though the vertical drop is steep, to make the run longer or shorter. At Sunshine, for example, the longest possible run is estimated at two and a half miles, while at Lake Louise a skier can stretch his run to well over a mile and a half.

Western Canadians don't have to go to the mountains to ski. When we counted them recently, Saskatchewan had thirteen separate ski resorts and Manitoba had eleven, none of them in real mountains. Alberta reported fifteen and of these at least half a dozen were outside of the mountain areas. I started my skiing at Tor Hill, four miles east of Regina, at a city park called Boggy Creek. Tor Hill has a recorded vertical drop of forty-five feet and ten years ago had no tows of any kind. We simply had to climb the hill, one ski over the next, before we got the thrill of a 700-foot run to the bottom. But that small hill got me and several hundred other prairie people hooked on the thrills of downhill skiing. And in a country noted for its flat plains too.

Motoring Long Ago

Roy Stanbrook came across a little book in his private collection the other day that reminded him of his first lengthy motor trip fifty years before. I've had a look at the little book and can confirm that he and an uncle, the late Sol Hadley, drove the 613 miles between Borden, Saskatchewan and Portage la Prairie, Manitoba between June 22 and June 24, 1926. That was a few months before Roy Stanbrook joined Modern Press where he worked for nearly half a century, until his retirement on New Year's Eve, 1976.

Roy recalls his uncle's car was a Buick of the variety then known as a sedan. The trip started near Borden, Saskatchewan where Roy had moved with his widowed mother to live with a second uncle. The first notation says they "passed through Borden at seven-thirty A.M." which suggests they got away to a good start. Uncle Sol kept them at the early starts, too. They drove 230 miles on the first day and spent the night at Lumsden, Saskatchewan. The next morning they left Lumsden at seven-fifteen A.M., spent the second night at Virden, Manitoba, and got away on the third leg of their trip at eight A.M.

The log book, written in great detail in the hand of a fourteen-year-old boy, draws some conclusions about the trip. The odometer of the car stood at 3,732 miles when they set out and read 4,345 at the end, indicating a total trip of 613 miles. They purchased a total of thirty-three gallons of gasoline along the way for a total expenditure of $12.73. This indicates gasoline in those days sold for an average of thirty-eight cents a gallon. There were eight stops for gasoline with the largest purchase being five gallons; several were only two gallons.

The late Sol Hadley had once farmed at Edwin, Manitoba near Portage, and he was apparently going back to his home area with his nephew in tow. From the look of it, school was just out and the boy was on the first round of a long summer vacation.

Old Streetcars

Regina buried its thirty-nine-year-old streetcar service one rainy day in September, 1950. As the final official car pulled away from Broad Street and College Avenue on the start of its last run, one old-timer rather sadly reminisced, "Blessed be the dead the rain rains on."

It was raining in Regina and it was raining in the hearts of many of the group of old-timers and newcomers, officials and friends, throughout the last "commemorative" streetcar run. No. 48, the sentimentally decorated car which made the final trip — from the Broad-College terminus to the car barns on North Albert Street, some two miles distant — had made the run before. Its total service, like that of many others also being retired as streetcars, exceeded 1,250,000 streetcar miles.

Many of the men and women who officially bid "good luck and good-bye" to the last car were among those who greeted the first to travel Regina streets on July 28, 1911. Oldest among them was ninety-six-year-old Robert Sinton, a former alderman who headed the city public-works committee which built the street railway. Records show that Mr. Sinton drove the last spike in the steel rail line before the first car started its initial run. He also switched the last switch just at ten A.M., when the final run began.

Three other old-timers recalled direct links with streetcar initiation to Regina. L. A. Thornton, as city engineer in 1911, directed the building of the line in preparation for the first car. Two original employees of the system were also along: G. Milnes, the chief clerk; and F. Otway, line foreman.

Although they were burying Regina's last streetcar officially, the final trip was no death march. From its beginning to end the journey took just twenty-eight minutes, allowing along the way for a formal stop at city hall for the mayor to board. Mayor Garnet Menzies pinned a colorful bouquet to the side of the car before he entered to join seven other members of city council, who began the run at its start.

Outside the official party which filled most of No. 48's fourty-eight seats, a few ordinary friends gained entry. Joe Diamond was along but then he was no ordinary passenger, although unofficially present. Joe says he rode the first scheduled run thirty-nine years ago and claims to still possess ticket number two sold that day in 1911.

Motorman Alex Blair, a comparative newcomer to the city's transportation system, drove the last car as representative of the more than 150 men who work for the system. Mr. Blair was president of division 588, Amalgamated Association of Street Electrical Railway and Motor Coach Employees of America (AFL). Officials from every department of the city-operated utility rode along with their boss, Graham McAra, superintendent. They included Andy Murray, assistant superintendent; chief inspector Jack McKenty; chief clerk G. Milnes; number one motorman F. Drake; line foreman F. Otway; master mechanic Frank McGuiness; and night foreman A. Tiefenbach. D. W. Houston, former street-railway superintendent who retired in 1945, headed the list of old-time conductors. Oldest among them was S. B. Sanders who retired in 1937 after twenty-five years service. A group of some thirty other old-timers followed the last tram in a new, modern motor bus and greeted her as she made her final run to the barns.

There was little solemnity and much hilarity as No. 48 clanged merrily on her homeward trip. At one downtown intersection, Motorman Blair jumped a red traffic light — everyone seemed to enjoy that. Some even smoked en route, quite contrary to existing street-railway regulations.

Along the downtown streets crowds stopped to watch, some even cheered, as the final car passed by. The words of a newspaper reporter who wrote about the first official run thirty-nine years before seem appropriate for the last: "From start to finish the journey was made with the utmost comfort. Not a mishap occurred."

Selling Newspapers

Old newspaper boys are a bit like old soldiers who never die. The newsboys don't even fade away; they just go on talking about it. Most of you will already have heard about a former newsboy who grew up to become prime minister of Canada.* He often talks about his newspaper selling days and seldom misses an opportunity to recall a conversation he once had with another prime minister, the late Sir Wilfrid Laurier, when Mr. Laurier stepped across First Avenue in Saskatoon to buy a copy of the morning newspaper from the then-young Diefenbaker, who had a selling stand on the corner across from what once was the downtown CNR railway station. The station is gone, but the former newsboy still recalls vividly the occasion and has recounted the event often.

I had lunch the other day with Dr. John Archer, who has just retired from being the first president of the University of Regina, and he recalled that he was once a subscription salesman for *The Western Producer*. He recalled that his newsboy experience occurred in 1939 when he was teacher at a rural school near Kipling, Saskatchewan. He had entered a contest sponsored by *The Western Producer*, and the first challenge was to add a series of numbers which occurred in a scramble in the newspaper. Several apparently reached the correct total because phase two of the contest required that they undertake to sell subscriptions to the newspaper and the one who sold the most would win the grand prize which

---

* Rt. Hon. J. G. Diefenbaker

was $1,100, a princely sum in those days. John Archer says the ten-day period ran from January tenth to twentieth, and his school then being closed because of the year-end vacation, he took off on snowshoes and by horse to travel the surrounding countryside. When the tally had been recorded, John Archer had sold 434 subscriptions and won the coveted $1,100. He recalls the runner-up sold only 343.

I too started my business career as a newspaper salesman. In about 1936 I became a carrier boy for *The Regina Daily Star,* a newspaper no longer published. I recall on one occasion selling papers on the street. It was an extra edition published in the summer of 1937 when the German airship, the LZ 129, which had been christened the Hindenburg, caught fire and was completely destroyed while making a landing at the Lakehurst, New Jersey naval station on its first trans-Atlantic crossing that year. It had made several successful crossings the year before.

That was over forty years ago, long before television, and many didn't even have a radio. It then was the custom for daily newspapers to bring out special or extra editions when there was an unusual news event and to sell the extra copies on the streets. Regular newspaper route boys were called in to help sell these. That was my only experience as a street salesman for newspapers but I still remember the excitement of the occasion. I recall racing down the street and shouting a garble which sounded all the world like "wuxtree, wuxtree, read all about it."

Wheat Pool Fieldman

In 1976, Howard Tyler marked completion of forty years' service to the farmers of western Canada through Saskatchewan Wheat Pool, and at age sixty-five retired, leaving a string of accomplishments and the satisfaction of having been a fieldman for the Wheat Pool longer than any other man but one.

Like most other fieldmen Howard Tyler was born on a farm and started work for the Pool buying grain. His father Walter Tyler had come to the Mikado district of Saskatchewan in 1911 from the United States to ranch. But the rancher went broke, as some still do, and the Tylers moved to Spalding and took up farming. A few years later Walter Tyler became a grain buyer for the old Co-op Elevator Company at Spalding and, when the Pool took over Co-op elevators, he transferred to the Pool. Howard Tyler was born at Spalding and grew up there, he and four sisters.

After completing high school he worked for a time in a general store at Spalding and in August 1935 joined the Wheat Pool as a helper in the country elevator at Spalding and later as an assistant agent. In the following five years he operated country elevators for the Pool at Tisdale, Watson, and Kelvington, and in August 1940 he joined the Canadian air force. He was trained as a wireless operator and air gunner, commissioned on graduation, and assigned to an Australian squadron in coastal command, patrolling the Atlantic Ocean from an air base at Leuchers near Dundee, Scotland. He flew on operations for two full years, mostly in the old Hampden aircraft which was

armed with aerial torpedoes. In time he earned a trip home
on leave, and that's when he got lost for the first time in his
life.

The way Howard recalls it, the Australians misplaced
his records as soon as he left for Canada, and the
Canadians were never told he had arrived back. After
several weeks on leave with his new wife, Pearl McDonald
of Rose Valley, Saskatchewan, he finally ran out of money
and took a job in a Montreal warehouse. Later they moved
to Rose Valley, and Howard managed a Co-op store while
he was still officially lost to the air force.

In 1945 Howard Tyler was found again, formally
discharged, and returned to the Wheat Pool on January 1,
1946, this time as a fieldman. When he retired he had
served in that role for thirty years, longer than any other
man except John Stratychuk. Mr. Stratychuk retired from
the Pool in 1968 after forty years of service with the Pool,
all of them in the field service. Howard Tyler served in the
field staff for both district six around Regina and district
fourteen in the northeast and in 1958 became field
supervisor. In 1960 he moved to head office and for several
years has been manager of field services.

Those thirty years have seen many changes in the role of
Wheat Pool fieldmen. In the beginning, Howard says
fieldmen were "agents of change," spending much of their
time helping individual farmers organize co-operatives to
meet their changing needs. Later, fieldmen became more
of an information group, listening to the problems of
farmers and trying to provide information to help in
solutions. Now, fieldmen spend more of their time helping
Pool delegates and local Pool committees grapple with the
problems. They operate training courses and briefing
sessions for others who in turn work directly with
individual farmers. As Tyler puts it, the need for this kind
of change in emphasis arose because problems are more
complex, and it became impossible for fieldmen to call on
as many farmers as they used to.

Howard Tyler played a major role in the changing

direction for Wheat Pool fieldmen. He also helped western farmers in many other ways. He was named by the Pool to the Board of Directors of Western Co-operative College when the college was first proposed about 1959 and became the second chairman of the board after Lewis L. Lloyd relinquished that post. Tyler was chairman during the difficult years of raising funds and building the new college buildings which were completed in 1962.

For many years he has been an active member of the Association of Co-operative Educators, an international association embracing members from Canada, the United States, and parts of South America. Some years ago ACE, as it is known, awarded him an Award of Merit "for [his] outstanding contribution to co-operative education and training."

A Quiet Revolutionary

Recent changes in the purpose and structure of the Co-operative Union of Canada have been of sufficient magnitude to constitute a kind of revolution, even if a quiet revolution. The principal revolutionary has been Breen Melvin of Regina, a quiet-spoken and non-violent man who has long been associated with Canadian co-operatives and who recently retired as national president of the CUC. The revolution was gradual and perhaps not evident to all members of the co-operative associations which together form the national CUC federation. But it produced a change in direction which has given the CUC more of an action-oriented purpose than the former contemplative and philosophical vista which many thought its main concern.

A report prepared for the CUC in 1972 suggested that Canadian co-operatives have come to recognize the necessity of a well-staffed and equipped national office in Ottawa "to meet the needs of member co-operatives in following national developments of special interest to co-operatives and their members." The suggestion was that the following needed attention:

• provision of services required by member co-operatives to keep them abreast of technological and legislative developments with apparent implications for co-operatives or their members;

• provision of leadership in development of appropriate policies for submission to governments;

• representation of member co-operatives both nationally and internationally.

During his tenure as national president Breen Melvin spearheaded CUC consideration and implementation of change. When Mr. Melvin stepped down as president he was succeeded by Donald Lockwood, also of Regina, vice-president of Saskatchewan Wheat Pool, the largest-membership co-operative in Canada.

Breen Melvin has retired from the presidency after serving in many capacities for more than a quarter century. He remains on the CUC board of directors as past-president. His service began in 1946 when the CUC asked him to Ottawa to organize the CARE program in Canada. He did that and remained to become full-time research secretary for the Co-operative Union and later national secretary and treasurer. He returned west in 1957 to become secretary of Co-operative Insurance Services, a full-time position he still retains. In 1961 he returned to CUC as an elected member of its board and in 1963 became national vice-president. He became president in 1967.

Breen Melvin has represented Canadian co-operatives abroad for a number of years and was for a time the only Canadian member of the executive committee of the International Co-operative Alliance, the world body for co-operatives. He has represented Canadian co-operatives at several meetings of the Organization of the Co-operatives of the Americas, the western hemisphere body of co-operatives.

Canada's Future

Grant Maxwell and Stephen Worobetz have at least two things in common: they were both born in rural Saskatchewan, and they both have an interest in helping the rest of us face the future.

Grant Maxwell was born at Plenty, Saskatchewan, started to study law at the University of Saskatchewan, and was diverted to become a journalist, first with Saskatoon radio station CFQC and then for several years with the Saskatoon *Star-Phoenix*. Some years later he began a new life with the Catholic Center in Saskatoon and in 1969 went to Ottawa to become an adviser to the Canadian Catholic Conference of Bishops.

In 1974 he undertook a unique assignment for the Catholic Bishops which he called Project Feedback and identified it as "a listening and reporting experiment in social journalism." During an eight-month period (October, 1974 to May, 1975) he travelled to all ten provinces and talked with some 750 citizens and local leaders in forty urban and rural communities. He asked a number of questions, recorded the responses, and drew some conclusions. Here are some of his questions along with his conclusions about the responses.

Question: What kind of society would you like to live in?

Conclusion: "From the Pacific to the Atlantic there were men and women who long for and work towards a more human social order — whether it be local or provincial, national or global."

Question: How do you feel about daily life?

Conclusion: "Canadians are learning that quality of life depends much less on the quantity of things than on the quality of relationships."

Question: How do you feel about religious leadership today?

Conclusion: "Critical comments outnumbered favorable remarks by more than two to one across Canada. Many, perhaps most critics felt separated from spiritual leaders, as if these leaders were cut off from the everyday lives of other people."

Question: Some people are searching for more meaning in life. What are your views?

Conclusion: "Everywhere I heard and saw much evidence of both spiritual hunger and religious indigestion."

Question: How do you feel about the future — say ten years from now?

Conclusion: "Many whom I interviewed made a distinction between what they hoped for and what they expected to happen ten years hence. Usually their hopes were considerably higher than their expectations. Apprehensions and hopes were almost equally evident; oftentimes in the same persons."

Mr. Maxwell said responses to his series of reports, which have been given wide distribution across Canada, have exceeded expectations.

Stephen Worobetz has followed a different life pattern as he sought to administer to the needs of others. He was born at Krydor, Saskatchewan, also studied at the University of Saskatchewan, and then took his doctor of medicine degree at the University of Manitoba. After graduate study he became a surgeon and set up practice in Saskatoon. He served from 1970 to 1976 as lieutenant-governor of Saskatchewan.

In 1977, Dr. Worobetz became the founding president of a new Canadian Club in whose establishment he has taken a leading role. There had been Canadian Clubs in Saskatoon before but both the men's club and the women's club failed to maintain support in the 1950s and 1960s and were discontinued. The new club already has 325 members, both men and women, and no fewer than 185 persons turned up for a founding meeting for which the present lieutenant-governor, the Honorable George Porteous, had agreed to be host.

The first Canadian Club was started in Hamilton, Ontario in 1893 by Charles R. McCullough, who became concerned about the low ebb to which Canadian awareness had sunk in the decade before the turn of the century. Within fifteen years his Canadian Club idea had swept across the country. In 1909 an Association of Canadian Clubs was organized in Montreal. In 1939 the association was formally incorporated by an act of Parliament which expressed the purpose of the Canadian Club: "To foster throughout Canada an interest in public affairs and to cultivate therein an attachment to Canadian institutions." Canadian Clubs tell new members they offer an opportunity to hear outstanding speakers, a chance to broaden one's horizons, and a sense of participating in a nationwide organization trying to promote Canadian unity. Membership is open to anyone who accepts these objectives.

There were once 100 Canadians Clubs in Canada but the number began to ebb with the advent of television. There now are forty-four across the country, and the number has begun to increase mainly because of the mounting concern of Canadians everywhere for the future of the country.

I can't help but believe there is a connection between the work of these two prairie sons. Mr. Maxwell has demonstrated that Canadians across the country are unsatisfied with much of what they experience around them and look forward to a future which gives more attention to the human values. Dr. Worobetz and those who have helped him organize this new club have concluded that a major concern of Canadians is about the future of their country.

Persons

A Town for Brothers

Delisle, Saskatchewan is certainly a town for brothers. It was named after four brothers, gave hockey the Bentley brothers, has a number of brothers still farming in the district, and is the anchor location in Saskatchewan of an unusual religious denomination called Brethren in Christ. It is also the home town of a former friend of mine named Danny Climenhaga and, when I went there in 1976, I met two of his brothers who still live in the district. I say Danny is a former friend because he was killed in an automobile accident while serving as his brother's keeper on a United Nations' assignment in faraway Kenya several years ago.

   The visit to Delisle was prompted by the secretary of the local wheat Pool committee, a farmer named Clarence Chizek, who invited my wife and me to dinner in the town hall to help the local committee and others mark the opening of a newly renovated country elevator. It was quite an affair indeed with more that 200 farmers and their wives sitting down to a chicken dinner, some speeches by visiting notables, and finally a local committee annual meeting. During the evening I got to know about the many brothers who have helped to make Delisle a brotherly place. I learned that Clarence Chizek has a brother George who also serves on the local committee. As a matter of fact there were four sets of brothers serving on the sixteen-member Wheat Pool committee at Delisle: Evan and Orville Climenhaga, Danny's older brothers; Gordon and Stan Hills; Lloyd and Howard Schumacher; and the Chizek brothers.

One of the visiting notables was Merv Ryan, director of Saskatchewan Wheat Pool's country-elevator division; his brother Howard was in the crowd at dinner. Merv said he had come from the district and had begun buying grain for the Pool many years ago at nearby Chambers' Siding.

Canadian National Railways built its Goose Lake branch line from Saskatoon to Rosetown in 1907-08, and the line ran through farmland owned by the four Delisle brothers, Amos, Eddie, Eugene, and Fred. The town was named in their honor.

William Bentley was another early settler, and the Bentleys had six sons and seven daughters. All six brothers took to hockey and Max, Doug, Reg, Wyatt (Scoop), Jack, and Roy all played for the Drumheller (Alberta) Miners in the late 1930s when that team won the western Canada senior hockey championship. Later Max and Doug went on to National Hockey League fame and played with the Chicago Black Hawks. Brother Reg joined them for a time, and the three Bentley brothers played on one line with the Hawks. Later Max moved to the Toronto Maple Leafs.

Another settler about that time was Ruben Climenhaga, the father of my friend Danny who was the youngest of a family of ten, five brothers and five sisters. Two of Danny's brothers still live at Delisle. Evan was chairman of the meeting and has been chairman of the local Wheat Pool committee for the last year.

The story of Ruben, father of the Climenhaga family of Delisle, is a fascinating one because it was he who introduced the Brethren in Christ church into Saskatchewan and founded at least four congregations. Apparently the sect originated in Germany about the beginning of the eighteenth century and, while formally called German Baptist Brethren, soon acquired the name of Dunkards after the German word *tunken* which means "to dip," because they believed in baptism by immersion. They are said to be similar to the Mennonites in their practices, rejecting infant baptism, denying themselves most worldly pleasures, and refusing to bear arms. The sect was believed to have immigrated to America about 1720, settling in several districts of Pennsylvania. One of the settlements became known as the River Brethren because they lived near the Susquehanna River in Lancaster County. About 1790 one of the Pennsylvania families moved to the Niagara Falls area of Ontario and established the first Canadian congregation. For a time the Canadian community was also known as the River Brethren, but in 1904 the official name of Brethren in Christ was chosen by the Canadian denomination.

Ruben Climenhaga moved west about 1911 and took up a homestead at Delisle. Later he also homesteaded at Paddockwood in northern Saskatchewan and established Brethren in Christ churches at Delisle and Paddockwood, at nearby Meath Park, and also at Kindersley.

Danny served during the Second World War overseas in the medical corps. My wife and I met him when he came to the University of Saskatchewan to study economics. Later he took graduate training at the University of London in England. He remained unmarried and took to United Nations service, serving on UN census projects in the Sudan, Jordan, and Afghanistan. He returned to Canada and lectured for a time on the Regina campus of the University but returned again to the UN for service on a population-control project in Kenya. He was killed on August 29, 1968 when struck down while crossing a street in Nairobi, the capital of Kenya.

My friend Danny Climenhaga would have been fifty-five this year, and I know he would have been proud to know that the brotherly traditions he learned from his father at Delisle have carried on into the next generation. His brother Evan and his wife have two sons: Robert has become a minister in the Brethren in Christ church at Niagara Falls, Ontario and Duane, who became an agricultural engineer at the University of Saskatchewan, has just begun a four-year assignment with the United Nations in Kenya.

Farmers' Country Meeting

Ted Turner, president of Saskatchewan Wheat Pool, said the grace and then scraped his chair across the floor like the rest of the ninety-three persons in the Borden (Saskatchewan) Community Hall one day in 1974 and tucked into a full-course turkey dinner with all the trimmings. It was high noon, and Turner and the rest were about to begin a Wheat Pool sub-district committee banquet, an annual event that makes the Wheat Pool different from many organizations in Canada and the role of its president unique in Canada if not in the world.

The hundreds of farmers across Saskatchewan who serve on Wheat Pool committees know the scene well. It happens every year in the spring, sometimes at noon and sometimes in the evenings, and the programs are usually the same: lunch or dinner, a slide presentation about some aspect of the Pool's activity or concerns, a speech by the local delegate or some visiting official, and a question period. Sometimes there is coffee after adjournment. There is always plenty of fun, sometimes a bit of heated argument, and usually some straight-forward talk. It's a time for Pool members to say what they think about their organization and an opportunity to discuss future policies and programs.

The Pool president is required to keep a rigorous schedule not shared by the presidents of most large organizations. He must first be a farmer. He faces three elections: first as delegate in his sub-district where all Pool members are electors, later for director where the ten or so delegates in each district are electors, and again as president where the sixteen directors are the electors. He must also meet Pool members on occasion at the country level for frank exchanges like those occurring here. Ted Turner has been doing it since 1957 when he became the Wheat Pool delegate for district sixteen, sub-district one which surrounds his family farm at Maymont in northwestern Saskatchewan.

There are 140 delegates, and they each hold annual banquet-conferences for committee members, the local farmers who have served for the year as representatives of Pool members and shareholders at their own delivery point. There are more than 800 committees, and membership averages about ten.

The meeting for Ted Turner was not much different than most of the others. Not much, but some different, and the difference was that the visiting delegate was Mr. E. K. Turner, the president of Saskatchewan Wheat Pool, a farmer co-operative with about 90,000 shareholders and 70,000 active patrons all of whom are shareholders, and whose enterprises make it one of Canada's biggest businesses. Pool enterprises include ownership and operation of country elevators with an annual handle equal to two-thirds of all farmer deliveries in the province of Saskatchewan; terminal elevators at the Lakehead and Vancouver, and shared ownership of other terminals which together handle about one-third of Canada's total grain export; farm service centers, supply warehouses, and bulk-fertilizer facilities to market a wide variety of farm supplies; livestock yards in Alberta and Saskatchewan and one in Ontario along with agency operations at other locations which together handle half the cattle and twenty per cent of the hogs marketed by Saskatchewan farmers; a flour mill; and a printing company. Along with this operation the Pool is part owner of a number of other co-operative enterprises including insurance, fertilizer manufacture, a grain-sales company, and vegetable-oil processing.

The purpose of the springtime committee banquet-conferences is two-fold: to thank local committee men for the long hours of unpaid activity they have undertaken during the year on behalf of their fellow farmers and to provide an opportunity at the local level for discussion of major questions facing farmers and farming. When the Wheat Pool president himself attends the meeting the discussion is always on a high plane, although the subject matter is little different from any other banquet-conference held across the province.

Lunch was served by the United Church Women and included roast turkey and cranberries, scalloped potatoes, salad, buns and butter, a choice of homemade pies (banana cream, Boston cream, coconut cream, chocolate, flapper) and plenty of coffee.

Farmers and their wives had driven to Borden that morning from their nearby farms or from countryside surrounding the towns and villages with names like Fielding, Lilac, Maymont, Radisson, Richard, and Ruddell. Some of them had braved country roads which threatened to be snow covered by nightfall as ground drift increased with a rising wind. One of their number was Franklin Mohler, a veteran seed grower from Maymont and a long-time neighbor of the Turners, both Ted and his father. Mr. Mohler recalled briefly his first brush with the idea of a Wheat Pool and said it had occurred at a meeting hastily called on the Turner farm, farmed by the father in 1924. He said at the time many who had attended that meeting were being pressed by grain merchants and by others, and wanted to find a way to improve their situation. He said young farmers who do not know firsthand about those days should listen when their fathers recall the great difficulties which beset farmers in the days when the Pool was founded.

Rummage Sales

Have you ever been to a rummage sale in the basement of a church? If any of you have not, I can assure you it is a fine old western Canadian tradition you ought not to miss when next the chance is offered. I was invited to visit a rummage sale for a sneak preview on the night before opening, and I jumped at the offer for two reasons: it had been years since I'd been to one and my recollections were getting foggy, and this particular sale was to occur in the basement of the Regina city church I knew very well in the years before the Second World War.*

I'd had dinner that night at the home of Dr. and Mrs. Jack Boan, long-time friends in Regina. Dr. Boan is an economist at the University of Regina and had to leave soon after the meal to lecture to an evening class. Mrs. Boan, who operates an antique shop in Regina, had offered her services to the ladies of the church to help them price items for the rummage sale. She asked me to go along and I readily agreed.

I want to tell you, a rummage sale the night before opening is a busy place. Tables everywhere with ladies and their husbands running around with cartons of donated goods as they arrived. Some husbands are shouting, "Where do I put this one?" One husband took an earned rest and came over to a table I was studying. He looked over the display quietly for some minutes and then asked, "Tell me, what is there here I simply can't live without?"

Living without is the key to all rummage sales. The

---

*First Presbyterian Church, Regina, Saskatchewan.

ladies of this church hold one every year, attract several
hundred shoppers Friday night and Saturday afternoon,
and raise something like $1,500 for the church. Only they
don't call their event a rummage sale but rather "an
opportunity sale."

The items for sale had been donated by the ladies of the
church themselves and were arranged in a dozen or so
departments. I spent more than an hour wandering about,
reviving memories on a number of counts.

The et cetera department: This one took my eye
immediately for it contained the castoffs of people who
apparently live the kind of life I have lived. There was a
basinette made out of wicker and painted several times, a
high chair, a stroller, two sleighs each with a box painted
red, all reviving memories of the days when I was a child.
Then there were tricycles and bicycles, three black-and-
white TV sets each with an antenna that was bent, an old
portable Singer sewing machine, four suitcases, a roll-
away bed, and even a hooked rug.

Specialties: This department was equally nostalgic.
There were napkin rings, pocket flasks covered with
leather, candle sticks of many kinds, and assorted knick-
knacks. There were ornaments representing owls, dogs and
elephants, airmen and soldiers, cats, squirrels, swans and
fish. There were several old tobacco pouches, some with
pipe cleaners and filters thrown in. There were also trays,
casserole dishes, cookie plates, lamps, and waste baskets.

Wall hangings: Discards from walls through at least half
a century and more were represented in the "home-sweet-
home" plaques, prayers, poems, and pictures. Some of the
frames were priceless but many of their contents had
become faded through age.

Jewelry: One table contained the priceless ornaments of
several generations, rings, pins, beads, and brooches.
There was even a grab-box special at this table: anything
in sight for only fifty cents!

Staples: It has been years since I heard that name used
in any other connection than food, but slowly I recalled

the staple section of that old departmental store. In this corner there were bedspreads, quilts, curtains, and doilies, table mats and dresser scarfs. Many of the items had been hand manufactured by women of another generation and sold for the first time also in aid of the church.

The room: The location in the church I used to know as the "ladies' parlor" had been named "the room," and it contained the fashionable items of this decade and the last. There were long, formal gloves, lingerie, evening gowns, street-length dresses, and even pant suits. Nearby were shorter gloves, hats, and purses of all kinds.

The commode: The best item of all was simply "the commode," and it attracted the largest crowd, even at the preview. It was a piece of furniture shaped like a cube and measuring about two feet along each side. It was made of oak and nicely varnished. All of us agreed it would have made a fine front-hall piece, somewhere one might expect to sit when putting on overshoes next winter. But the most startling thing of all was that its original purpose had been perfectly preserved: the white porcelain pottie was fully operational and in place. Mrs. Boan said it ought to bring between twenty-five and fifty dollars, and I'll bet it did.

It was a wonderfully nostalgic evening, and I was told later the sale went as expected, clearing out most of the treasures in record time.

Mainstreeting

Mainstreeting as practised by some western Canadians has become an art. For those of you who do not know what it is, mainstreeting is walking down the main street of your favorite town from one end to the other, waving at everyone you see, stopping to talk to a few, and dropping in occasionally on open doorways to say hello to shopkeepers. The Right Honorable John Diefenbaker, former prime minister of Canada, helped to make mainstreeting into an art when he lived in Prince Albert, and he returns there every so often to take a stroll along Central Avenue, which is Prince Albert's main street.

When in Toronto I often call on Godfrey Hudson, an old friend from out west, and we usually get to chatting about mutual acquaintances. The name of John Diefenbaker was mentioned not long ago, and that brought up the subject of mainstreeting, and then Godfrey said, "You know, I'd really like to take a mainstreeting walk down Second Avenue in Saskatoon, all the way from the offices of *The Western Producer* to the Legion hall at the southern end." And then he added, "But I don't suppose I ever will."

I'd like to tell you something about why he doubts he'll make that walk again. As some of you might expect, Godfrey Hudson is an old newspaper colleague. He was born on a farm at Tuberose, near Kyle, Saskatchewan, where his parents, Mr. and Mrs. Eadric H. S. Hudson, were homesteaders. Godfrey took an arts degree at the University of Saskatchewan in the 1940s and joined radio station CFQC in Saskatoon as a newsman. In time he became news director, and I recall made an exceptionally good job of it for more than a decade. He married Stephanie Gunnlaughson whose Icelandic parents, Mr. and Mrs. Olgeir Gunnlaughson, farmed at Wynyard and later Melfort where the Hudsons lived for a time. They have three teen-aged sons, Kenneth, Richard, and Timothy.

The Hudsons moved east where Godfrey worked first as a radio editor with Press News, the radio news arm of The Canadian Press, moved on to become a reporter for *The Globe and Mail* in Toronto, and then news director for radio station CKEY in Toronto. A few years ago Godfrey came down with what was diagnosed as cancer in his leg and in time, after several operations, he was rid of the cancer but lost all of his right leg, right up to and including the hip bone. This may be considered inconvenient, but it can also be nearly disastrous because the loss of this huge bone area has meant three things:

• He doesn't have enough leg to hang an artificial limb on and he must be satisfied with crutches.

• There is not enough rump left for a satisfactory seat, and he must sit partly on one side of his rump and lean on an arm chair with his elbows.

• The loss of so much bone marrow has reduced his body's capacity to produce the required red blood corpuscles, and he doesn't have enough energy for a normal day of activity and must sleep frequently during the day.

You'd never believe all of these difficulties when you visit him because he has remained cheerful through the years. But recently a new difficulty has arisen. His constant use of crutches has apparently contributed to development of some form of growths in his hands which, when the pressure of the crutch is placed upon them, become very painful. Now he must restrict his walking too.

And that brings me back to his wish about mainstreeting down Second Avenue in Saskatoon. I'm quite certain he could manage the walk with the help of some friends and maybe some rest stops along the way if only he could get to Saskatoon. But an automobile trip would be too exhausting and normal air travel might be also. He would require an aircraft with a bed and no change-overs en route. I don't know whether it is possible to arrange such a trip, but I thought I'd tell you about it.

Accidents Do Happen

I know of few other accomplishments that have captured the imagination of men and women like that of human flight. I've come to know several who have accomplished this skill in recent years, and without exception they speak with a special kind of glow about the wonder of their first solo flight. Experienced pilots tell me the wonder never ceases and that they experience the thrill anew each time they become fully airborne on a new flight.

I have no idea how many Canadians have learned to fly since the first powered flight in Canada was accomplished by the late J. A. D. McCurdy near Baddeck in Nova Scotia on February 23, 1909. But I do know that on April 1, 1975 Canada reported 44,745 licensed pilots of all kinds and that 31,630 of them held private licenses. I learned these last two details from Wilf Brandt who farms not far from Regina and is past-president of the Flying Farmers of Saskatchewan. Wilf said there were about 3,600 flying farmers in Canada, that 650 of them live in Saskatchewan, and that most flying farmers own their own aircraft. He also said that on April 1 there were 10,862 privately owned aircraft registered in Canada. Julien Audette, manager of the Regina Flying Club, told me there are twelve flying training schools in Saskatchewan.

I've produced this kind of data about flying to demonstrate that men and women do want to fly and are doing what is necessary to get themselves aloft. Now I want to comment on three persons who were killed the other day in an air crash while they were returning from a vacation flight in their own aircraft. What caused the single-engined monoplane to crash was not determined, but it was off course on a flight from Minot, North Dakota to Regina and had run into bad weather. Gordon Mitchell, the pilot, his wife Barbara, and their thirteen-year-old son Jamie died in the crash said to have occurred sometime during the evening of August 24 or early August 25, 1975 in a heavily wooded section of Moose Mountain Provincial Park in southern Saskatchewan.

Gordon Mitchell was among the most careful and meticulous of men I have ever known. He was trained first as a dentist, then studied orthodontia, and went to Regina about 1955 to practise orthodontics, which is a branch of dentistry concerned with the prevention and correction of irregular teeth, abnormal bite, and the bad effects of these on health, chewing, and facial appearance. I came to know these careful skills firsthand when he undertook the care of irregular teeth belonging to our two sons, and their regular grins now are everlasting tribute to his success. I also know some of the men with whom he often ventured into the northern lakes in search of relaxation and fish, and I have often heard them speak of his untiring attention to the smallest detail, an attention which brought for him the loving label of "mother Mitchell."   •

I have since learned that he took equal care of his flying machine. He had acquired whatever qualification is required for night flight and had provided the necessary equipment to ensure safety. I'm also told that one of the accomplishments of his recent vacation flight into eastern Canada had been to provide an opportunity for his wife Barbara, not herself a pilot, to learn how to land the plane should an emergency develop.

All of the above aside, I suppose the real reason I chose to write about the Mitchells was to add my few words as a memorial to three very human and sincere persons whose living touched the lives of a great many people indeed. I attended the memorial services in Regina and the huge mid-town church was packed to overflowing. Among those who paid tribute by their presence were:

• The families of Gordon and Barbara. Gordon had been born at Milestone where his father, the late Jim Mitchell, operated Mitchell's store as had his father before him. Gordon's mother, Mrs. Audie Mitchell, was there and so were his sister, Mrs. Margaret Ross of Moose Jaw, and his brother Bradley of Nanaimo, British Columbia, Barbara came from the East, and her father Mr. Henry M. Blaiklock of Toronto was there.

• The dentists of Saskatchewan whom Gordon had served for twenty years as colleague and official at local, provincial, and national levels.

• The friends from St. Stephen's Presbyterian Church, the suburban congregation they had helped to form and served in many ways.

• The uniformed boys from the Fifty-Ninth Boy Scout group whom Gordon had served as cubmaster and member of the local group committee. Jamie had been both a Cub and a Scout in that group.

• Julien Audette and the other members of the Regina Flying Club who had joined in the search for the aircraft.

• The disabled and the handicapped whom Barbara had helped in many ways through her support for Marina Creations which sold their work.

• Skiers young and old whom both Mitchells had helped through the many hours of instruction they had offered beginners through the Regina Ski Club.

The Rev. Harrold Morris, the Presbyterian minister who spoke at the memorial service, summed up the lives of the Mitchells when he said, "They seemed to get the greatest pleasure out of helping others to get pleasure." The Mitchells had two children. Their daughter Catherine, then eighteen, survived because she had stayed at home to plan her university courses which were to begin within a few days. I know after the shock wears away she will come to appreciate the unique contribution her parents made to others in the many ways in which they showed they cared.

Music Festivals

I sat in a banquet room the other night with 200 or so others and listened with fascination as more than forty speakers from across Saskatchewan went forward one by one to thank Gordon Hancock for the contribution he made over a generation to the musical life of the province. It was formally billed as a testimonial dinner for Mr. Hancock who, in 1976, retired as executive director of the Saskatchewan Music Festival Association. The speakers were mainly representatives of the forty-two music-festival organizations across the province, more than half of which he had helped to establish during his eighteen years as "mister music festival." As a permanent tribute, the Saskatchewan Music Festival Association announced establishment of the Gordon Hancock Music Scholarship which will be available for "serious music students only." At the outset the scholarship will be awarded to the best pianist judged at the Saskatchewan festivals; later the scholarship may be extended also to singers and performers on brass, strings, and woodwinds.

When his turn came to respond Gordon Hancock said he was "thrilled to pieces" by the entire evening which he had found to be "complete and heart warming." He said he was overjoyed and added with characteristic modesty he was "thankful of the opportunity to serve you all."

I'm not much of a musician, but everywhere I turned over the years I found the Hancocks making music, helping others to appreciate music, and giving leadership to community endeavors related to music.

• Gordon and Mossie were both performing artists of

considerable accomplishment and often appeared on the recital stage or on radio as either solo or dual pianists.

• For sixteen years they conducted together two radio programs over station CKCK in Regina which found wide appeal across the southern half of the province. On both programs they played records from their personal collection. One program was called "As You Like It" and the other "The Music of Man."

• Both Gordon and Mossie taught piano students for several years from the studios of the Regina Conservatory of Music. Many of their students won honors in festivals in Saskatchewan and elsewhere. Both served as adjudicators on the festival circuit across Canada.

• Gordon Hancock was a member of the Rotary Club in North Battleford and Regina for thirty years and was usually to be found as club pianist. In Regina he was also active in the Rotary Club's Christmas carol festival at which he often was both accompanying organist and master of ceremonies.

• He was choirmaster and organist for several churches. Before leaving his home town of Saskatoon he was organist and choirmaster for St. James Anglican Church for several years; at North Battleford he held the same positions with Third Avenue United Church and after moving to Regina served for several years in similar positions with Metropolitan United Church which later became Knox-Metropolitan Church.

But the warmth and generosity of the statements made by the large group of people from across the province that night arose more from the warmth and generosity of Gordon Hancock himself than from his fine record of accomplishments. One by one, each spoke of the encouragement he had given as they had struggled to establish a local music festival and of the generosity and understanding with which he had adjudicated some of the youngsters often appearing in competition for the first time.

Gordon Hancock was born in 1912 at Stoke-on-Trent in Staffordshire in England where his parents were both employed in pottery works. His father was office manager of a pottery and his mother was what Gordon described as a journeywoman painter; her job was to paint designs on the finished pottery. When he was but an infant his family moved to Canada and settled in Saskatoon where his father became engaged as an accountant with the bridge and building department of what later became Canadian National Railways.

Gordon showed musical talent at a tender age and began music lessons when he was only five. By the time he was ten he had discovered the studio of Dr. Lyle Gustin, known across the province as the dean of piano teaching. For several years he studied under Gustin and also Reginald Bedford and in time became an associate of the Toronto Conservatory of Music. Later he took the licentiate in music and the fellowship diploma from Trinity College of London, England.

In 1939 he was married to Mossie McCrae, the daughter of Dr. and Mrs. J. R. McCrae. Her father was a practising chiropractor in Lloydminster. In 1943 the Hancocks moved to North Battleford, then on to Regina in 1948.

Aside from his busy round in Saskatchewan he found opportunity to serve also in a wider community. From 1958 until 1976 he represented Saskatchewan on the Federation of Canadian Music Festivals and was national president from 1968 to 1970. He has been a member of the Administrative Council of the National Music Festival since it was founded in 1972. Recently he was named honorary representative from Saskatchewan on the Canadian Bureau for the Advancement of Music.

An Amazing Record

The Honorable Emmett Matthew Hall was approaching what most men would consider normal retirement age when, at age sixty-four, he was named to the Supreme Court of Canada. After more than twelve years he retired from that court, and although well over seventy-five appears and acts more agile and able than many men half his age.

Emmett Hall was born at St. Columban, Quebec and had become fluently bilingual before he completed grade school. He moved to Saskatoon with his parents to complete schooling, entered the University of Saskatchewan to study law, and graduated in the class of 1919 numbering among his classmates the Right Honorable John Diefenbaker, the prime minister who named Mr. Justice Hall to the Supreme Court of Canada. For a number of years he practised law in Saskatoon and lectured at the university's law school. He was a busy layman as well. For many terms he was chairman of the separate school board of Saskatoon, chairman of St. Paul's Hospital in Saskatoon, adviser to the Dominion Catholic Hospitals Conference, and president of the Saskatchewan division of Canadian Red Cross. He was active in the law society and the Knights of Columbus.

In a recent conversation he reported on his early activity on behalf of farmers. The first case he argued before the Supreme Court as a young lawyer was for prairie grain farmers in 1928, and he won. Another incident occurred in 1931 when he worked through one night to draft the agreement by which Saskatchewan Wheat Pool purchased a near-bankrupt newspaper from its three founders and took over publication of *The Western Producer.*

In 1951 his career took the kind of turn many lawyers seek as goal, and he became a judge, first as a member of the Saskatchewan Court of Appeal. In 1957 he became chief justice of the Court of Queen's Bench of Saskatchewan and, four years later, was returned to the Court of Appeal as its chief justice and was also named Chief Justice of Saskatchewan. He went to the Supreme Court in 1962, and he served Canada's most senior court with distinction until his voluntary retirement in 1973, a few months before compulsory retirement would have overtaken him at age seventy-five.

Despite his distinguished career it has been his contribution as a problem solver which has given him a special place in the Canadian history books. In 1962 he accepted appointment as chairman of a federal royal commission on health services and took on the study of Canada's needs for a medical health plan. The Hall report formed the basis for introduction of Canada's present national health programs. Since then he has directed two major studies relating to the future of education. In 1968 he was chairman of a commission in Ontario to study the aims and objectives of education in that province, and the report his commission brought forward called for integration of English and French language in Ontario schools and provided the basis for reorganizing much of the Ontario school system. In 1974 he directed a study for the Saskatchewan government which resulted in reorganization of the existing two-campus university system into two separate universities, the University of Saskatchewan and the University of Regina. Later he completed two other major activities, neither directly related to education or health but each of extreme importance to the future of all Canadians. He was the one-man commissioner who developed an acceptable contract settlement for railway workers who forced the national rail tie-up in 1974. That same year he concluded a study of the judicial system of Saskatchewan.

I have just finished reading this latter study, and it contains many observations which indicate the special concerns of this unusual man for his fellows, especially his fellows who may be less fortunate. I'll cite only one passage in which Mr. Justice Hall considers why we have courts of law. This is what he says:

> Briefly put courts exist to protect the rights, liberties and freedoms of citizens, otherwise these rights, liberties and freedoms would exist only in a vacuum. They do not speak for themselves to proclaim that they are fundamental and basic. Neither the Canadian Bill of Rights nor the Saskatchewan Bill of Rights are self-enforcing nor is any other statute or law.
>
> The courts are civilized society's substitute for the naked power of force. The prime purpose of courts is the impartial adjudication of disputes and the maintenance of public order without resort to violence.

In 1975 Mr. Justice Hall was named chairman of a five-man commission of inquiry charged by the federal government with designing a rational system of grain handling and transportation for the prairie area.

Man at the Center

Some jobs are more difficult than others and some people are better suited to take on the difficult than are their fellows. I can think of no more important job at this difficult juncture of Canadian history than that of being deputy minister of finance in the federal government, and I can think of no one better suited than the man who took that position in 1975. His name is T. K. Shoyama, and he is known affectionately to his many friends and acquaintances across Canada either as "Tommy" or as "Shoy." I'd like to discuss for a few minutes his peculiar suitability for a job that has scarcely ever been more difficult.

Those who understand how governments work will appreciate that the finance department is at the heart of the matter. Its primary function is described in the *Canada Year Book* as "responsible for advice to the government on the economic and financial affairs of Canada." The deputy minister is the senior public official and is responsible, in effect, for the operation of the department's six parts: tax policy; federal-provincial relations and economic programs; tariff, trade, and aid; international finance; financial operations; and long-range economic planning.

I suggest this is a difficult time in Canadian history: some Canadians are concerned about minorities and especially the problem of melding the minority French to the predominantly English culture; some are worried about the alienation of the more distant parts of the country, especially the West; some are upset about the energy crisis and pollution of the environment; and most

of us are in a quandry about how to meet ever-rising prices
of everything.

The choice of Thomas K. Shoyama at this time is
especially suitable.

He knows about minorities: Mr. Shoyama was born of
Japanese ancestry in British Columbia in 1918 and, along
with the other Japanese in British Columbia, was moved
from coastal areas to an internment camp in the British
Columbia interior. Later he served in the Canadian
army.

He understands the West: He moved to Saskatchewan
soon after the government of Premier Douglas took office
in 1944 and by 1949 was secretary to the provincial
cabinet's planning committee, a position he held for fifteen
years. He was an assistant deputy minister of finance in
1973 when the prime minister asked him to co-ordinate the
federal government's position for the Western Economic
Opportunities Conference at Calgary in 1973.

He is an energy specialist: In 1974 he was named deputy
minister of the federal department of energy, mines, and
resources where he took over one of the most difficult jobs
in the country, trying to resolve a number of questions
relating to the so-called energy crisis. He was the chief
federal planner for the recent federal-provincial agreement
on establishing oil prices for Canada.

He is an experienced economist: Mr. Shoyama took a
bachelor of commerce degree at the University of British
Columbia and later did graduate training in economics at
McGill. He has been a practising economist all of his adult
life, both in the provincial and federal public service and
as senior economist with the Economic Council of Canada
between 1964 and 1967 before moving to the federal
finance department.

He is a diplomat: Unlike some public servants who
know all the answers before they have heard the question,
Tommy Shoyama listens quietly, prods if he thinks the
whole story is not being told, grasps the guts of what is
being said quickly and thoroughly, and responds quietly

and with diplomatic consideration. He is not likely to be dogmatic about anything.

I would think this a good move for Canada to have such an understanding and informed public servant placed in this major role at this time in Canadian history. And those of us in the West can take heart that finally we have knowledge that one of the men in the center knows a lot about our problems and the issues which encourage a sense of alienation.

French Heifers

Times do change. When I was a boy I was told that all North Americans wanted to go to France to see the girlie shows and that French "chorines" (that's slang for chorus girls) were considered the best in the world. As a matter of fact the first time I went to Paris, which was about twenty years ago, I dropped into *Les Folies Bergère,* the place where the best show on earth was said to be, to check it out for myself. And I learned all that I had heard was correct. I then knew what they meant when they sang that First World War song, "How ya gonna keep 'em down on the farm? (after they've seen Paree.)"

Now they go to France to look at the heifers. One day in 1975, I had a conversation with Larry Bingham of Cut Knife, Saskatchewan about a week he spent in France looking over the heifers before coming home with an order for his choice among the best of the Maine-Anjou breed. For anyone who may not know, Maine-Anjou cattle are among the largest of the European breeds, are said to gain rapidly, and look something like big red-and-white Shorthorns.

He flew from Saskatoon directly to Paris and after only an hour or two in the airport of that great city took off for the provinces of Maine and Anjou to keep an appointment with a representative of the Maine-Anjou herd book. He didn't get to a single show in Paris, and they kept him so busy down in the provinces that he didn't get to any there either. But he told me he had a successful trip and flew home a week later quite satisfied. What he did was visit countless farms with a representative of the Maine-Anjou herd book, examine heifers available for purchase, and selected as his first choice "Joline." He expects her to arrive in Canada in the spring. He also selected a second choice in case the first gets turned back.

Larry is twenty-six, took a degree in agriculture from the University of Saskatchewan, and joined his father Fred Bingham on the home farm which they operate as a partnership. They crop wheat, barley, and rapeseed on the 1,200 cultivated acres, and they both have cow-calf and feeder-beef operations. They had specialized in Angus, Herefords, and Shorthorns but plan to have Joline, the new Maine-Anjou heifer, bred artificially.

Going to France for a purebred heifer is no small matter. Like the many Canadians who have gone before him and since, Larry Bingham had to plan ahead and had to have a generous cheque book handy. The trip itself cost him about $1,000; he paid $6,800 for Joline, and he'll put up a further $4,000 or so to finance her trip to Canada, an amount which includes quarantine charges.

Gazebos

I'd never even heard of the word "gazebo" until a few weeks ago, and then this summer I finally got to see one. I was invited to a party to mark the coming out of a gazebo or, if you like, the launching of one. At least that's what the host thought it might be until some of his guests turned the tables on him and made the occasion his, rather than the gazebo's.

In case you didn't know, a gazebo is a free-standing structure, a kind of building that looks much like the old summer house. The gazebo I met stands in the backyard behind the home of Roy and Gwen Stanbrook in Saskatoon and has a roof and screened walls. It is an ideal place in which to sit on a summer evening and avoid the mosquitos.

Well, the Stanbrooks told everyone that the party was to launch the gazebo, and that confused many because some had never seen one before and some had never even heard the name. But after a generous lunch, things got a bit out of hand, and some friends with long memories produced a huge cake with some fancy icing writing that said something like "happy anniversary to Gwen and Roy." Then the truth came out: the occasion was really the fortieth anniversary of their marriage.

Roy Stanbrook was the most senior of all of the men and women who help to publish *The Western Producer* and operate Modern Press. He joined the company on April 11, 1927 when he was a mere boy and remained with the original company after it was purchased on June 1, 1931 by Saskatchewan Wheat Pool. Modern Press was then located elsewhere in Saskatoon, but a few months after Roy Stanbrook joined, the company moved into new quarters on Second Avenue North where it remained all of the intervening forty-eight years.

At his retirement, Roy Stanbrook was the only remaining employee of Modern Press who was with the company when it was purchased by the Wheat Pool, and for a number of years he was one of its senior employees. Through the years Roy Stanbrook has come to be known around the plant as "Mr. Modern Press" and across western Canada as the dean of the printing industry. For a number of years he occupied the senior position in the printing operation and more recently was business manager for the entire operation, responsible both for the printing company and the business side of *The Western Producer*. He retired at age sixty-five on December 31, 1976.

But I started out to talk about the gazebo and the wedding anniversary for the Stanbrooks and not about Mr. Stanbrook's working world. Roy and Gwen were married in Saskatoon on August 5, 1935 and except for service during the Second World War have lived in Saskatoon continuously. They have a son, Douglas, who lives in Burnaby, British Columbia, and a daughter, Muriel, who lives in Winnipeg. They also have two grandchildren.

Gazebos are quite interesting in themselves and certainly their launching is a valid reason for a delightful mid-summer garden party. But even more interesting is a party which turns out to be a fortieth wedding anniversary. That's really unusual. And the unusualness is compounded when the participants to that anniversary are able to say they have remained in one city most of that time and with the one employer for nearly half a century.

Octogenarians

Some men and women are able to pack a whale of a lot of living into sixty years, even sixty years of married life. Mr. and Mrs. Alexander McAlpine Boan are just such a couple, and they have lived together in or near the village of Briercrest, Saskatchewan for sixty years. Mr. Boan, then a farmer at Briercrest which is near Moose Jaw, was married on January 10, 1917 to Dorothy Goldthorpe Holtby, a young school teacher who had come to Briercrest from her home in Lloydminster, Saskatchewan.

Some may not believe sixty years is much of a landmark and, by itself, it may not be. But this unusual couple have made more of their sixty years married than many, and they continue to serve their community and their neighbors through church and community activities. Consider the following accomplishments:

Between 1933 and 1972 Mrs. Dorothy Boan had served the Briercrest Rural Telephone Company both as business agent and switchboard operator. She retired from both positions in the spring of 1972 when Sask Tel took over the local co-operative company, one of the last on the prairies to join the government network. Mrs. Boan then was seventy-seven and had served as operator on the old-time manual switchboard for thirty-nine years, and before that had also served the local company for five years as secretary.

Alex Boan signed on with the same rural telephone company during the Second World War as its only lineman and served until 1972 when the company joined the Sask Tel network. He was mad as a hatter too when they made him quit the lineman's job before winter set in, to prevent any accidents while the local company was being transferred to Sask Tel. Mr. Boan then was 85 years old and let it be known that he could climb a telephone pole as well as any lineman they had.

When Mrs. Boan gave up the telephone job she also retired as circulation agent for the *Leader-Post,* a position she had filled for forty-three years, and for much of that time she had been local correspondent as well. Four of her five children had been *Leader-Post* carriers at Briercrest, a record by itself. The Boans have three sons and all three, together with the father, serve the Presbyterian church as elders.

The Boan couple took to square dancing in 1970 when Mr. Boan was 83 years old and since have danced regularly throughout the winter and have participated in international square dance competitions at Prince Albert and Regina in Saskatchewan; Brandon in Manitoba; and Williston, North Dakota.

Alexander McAlpine Boan was born on the family homestead near the east end of Buffalo Pound Lake, in what later became Saskatchewan, on January 27, 1887. His parents, Mr. and Mrs. David Boan, had established their homestead the year before and stayed on to raise a family of twelve, eight sons and four daughters. Most of the Boan family took to farming and most remained in Saskatchewan. Besides Alex, five survive.

Dorothy Goldthorpe Holtby was born on June 12, 1894 in England and came to Canada with her parents, Mr. and Mrs. Robert Holtby, who settled at Lloydminster in 1903 as Barr colonists. She studied to be a teacher at North Battleford and took up her first school at Briercrest where she met Mr. Boan. There were five children in the Holtby family but only Dorothy survives.

The Boans themselves had five children. Dr. John Alexander Boan of Regina is professor of economics at the University of Regina and for many years was head of the economics department there. He is married to the former

Jean Campbell of Saskatoon. Jean McDougall Boan married William T. Dix of Winnipeg. David Robert Boan married Mabel Zimmerman of Dunville, Ontario and went into business in that town. Zaida Dorothy Boan married Raymond Guilchrist of Maple Creek, and they now live near Duncan, British Columbia where Mr. Guilchrist is a land appraiser. Douglas Bruce Boan is a physician and practises medicine near Nanaimo, British Columbia. He was married to the former Peggy Petrescu of LaFleche, Saskatchewan. There are also fourteen Boan grandchildren and five great-grandchildren.

These two senior citizens have contributed greatly to the life and times of western Canada and face the future together with a zest and vigor not often found in octogenarians, one of whom was going on to ninety.

Builder of Bridges

Alexander Russell Cameron was for most of his adult life a newspaperman. Sometimes he would even agree to being called an historian for history was his main intellectual interest. But he will be remembered mainly as a "builder of bridges," a task for which he would modestly never claim any expertise. The bridges he built during most of his sixty-six years were figurative and not physical; they were between yesterday and today, between the old and young, between the possible and the probable.

The minister who spoke at his funeral in 1970 said his life had fulfilled the ancient precept first spoken by Moses, who warned the Israelites that when they crossed the River Jordan into the promised land they must take with them the stones on which were written the ancient laws, and, in the new land, they must always show respect for the old law. The stones on which Alexander Russell Cameron carved the record and his interpretation of it were many: the newsprint of a journalist, the film of a skilled photographer, and the stacks and displays of first the librarian and then the museum director. In his time he played a great many parts.

During his early school days in Ontario, through high school and Normal school in Saskatoon, while he taught in rural schools throughout Saskatchewan from 1923 to 1931, and during his university career, he was known as Russell Cameron. Many who came to his funeral nearly forty years after he had changed his name to Alex spoke only of Russ Cameron.

Alex Cameron was neither intense nor casual about his

friendships and acquaintances, but many who knew him only slightly considered they knew him well. He helped to make this possible by devoting full attention to any query directed towards him and never treating one person with less personal respect than another. When he formally retired as a senior official of Saskatchewan Wheat Pool, a group of secretaries and stenographers who had come to know him through the years invited him as their guest to a luncheon party. It was one of the retirement events he recalled with the greatest of warmth. And so did each of the dozen girls who were his hostesses.

His working life was devoted to recording the facts in word and picture and to seeking an interpretation of their meaning for those around him. Following his university graduation in 1933 (in English and History) he was a newspaperman for two full decades, partly as a reporter but mainly as an interpreter and an editorial writer. Most of his newspaper career was spent with the Saskatoon *Star-Phoenix* where he was associate editor for more than a decade. In 1953 he joined Saskatchewan Wheat Pool where he remained until his retirement in 1969. For many years he was director of the Pool's publicity department. He was also responsible for administration of the Pool's lending library which was one of the first of its kind in the province, making available to farmers a selection of good reading through a mailed lending service. The lending library was discontinued about the time of Mr. Cameron's retirement in 1969.

As an indication of his bridge-building activities while at the Wheat Pool, the Saskatchewan Weekly Newspaper Association named him in 1966 to be their first "honorary printer's devil" and presented him with some type slugs embedded in a plastic paper weight. A printer's devil is the term for an apprentice printer. The weekly editors said the honor was to thank Mr. Cameron for his many years of assistance and service to the province's weeklies while he was director of publicity for the Wheat Pool.

Throughout his active writing career, he also devoted energy and skill to photography, and his color pictures, mainly of Saskatchewan scenes, have been widely used on material printed by the Wheat Pool. He was particularly skillfull at photographing in natural color the native prairie.

Mr. Cameron had been a member of the board of the Western Development Museum since 1957 and its chairman since 1966. He was chairman at the time of his death, and since his retirement had devoted many hours at meetings of the museum board and with government officials trying to find a way to expand the museum's revenue so that it could improve its facilities for displaying the many reminders of early prairie settlement which are its particular interest.

The many other associations to which Alex Cameron devoted time, energy, and skill in his long bridge-building career all attest to his interest in helping his fellows to understand events of the past and present and interpret them for the future. He was an active officer at various times of the Saskatchewan Educational Television Association, the Canadian Institute of International Affairs, the Regina Library Association, the Community Chest of Saskatoon, the Saskatchewan Diamond Jubilee and Centennial Corporation, and the United Nations Association of Regina of which he was president at the time of his death.

Scottish-Styled Individualist

Dan Cameron was in all respects a philosopher for most of his eighty-three years. Some called him a musician but he was really a musical philosopher. Three decades with Regina's music life had elevated him to the unofficial title of "dean" and most certainly to a senior statesman's role. Those years spanned revolutions of life and mode in the city's musical world and touched on almost every facet of the community's cultural life.

His occupation was really music. In 1922 he joined the staff of the Regina Conservatory of Music, then a part of Regina College, as a teacher of voice and when he retired in 1951 had been director of the conservatory for twelve years. After formal retirement he continued to teach voice until his death in 1963, although in his final decade he also joined the *Leader-Post* as a full-time editorial writer. He wrote music notes for the *Leader-Post* for at least two decades and for much of that time wrote a weekly column on music. For twenty-five years he was choir director at Knox United Church.

A former provincial president of the Saskatchewan Registered Music Teachers Association, he was instrumental in its formation and active in its work for most of its existence. He was for many years a member of its examining board and represented the provincial body in the Canadian Federation of Music Teachers Associations as a national vice-president.

Quite apart from his professional music activity, he was a friend, director, and critic of Regina's amateur musicians for all of his three decades. For twenty years he conducted

the Regina Male Voice Choir. At various times he was also
conductor of the Ladies' Bach Choir, the Regina Amateur
Operatic Society, and the Regina Philharmonic Society.
He was among the first judges to adjudicate student
contestants in radio station CKCK's annual scholarship
auditions and remained until his death an adviser to the
event. He aided and judged similar talent-seeking projects
sponsored by many service clubs. For many seasons he
directed the annual Christmas carol festival presented by
the former R. H. Williams department store. He was a
veteran member of the organization which produces the
city's annual musical festival.

There was, however, another man, one not so well
known to the public eye — the Scottish-styled individual-
ist, the scholar, and the philosopher. Daniel Alexander
Cameron was born in Ottawa in 1880 of Scottish parents.
He was educated in Ontario and began his musical career
there as a teacher of voice and a conductor of church
choirs. His career was interrupted during the First World
War with service overseas, during which time he distinguished himself in the field by winning the Military Cross
for gallantry and being promoted to the rank of major.
Following his retirement from the army he served briefly
with the new post-war department of veterans affairs in
Ottawa before returning to music, his vocation.

Music was called his vocation and not his love, for
another study occupied his most cherished thoughts. That
major love, literature, formed the backdrop for his daily
living, where most of the walls of his residence were
literally book covered. Since he first learned to read,
"Dan" — the name by which those who knew him best
called him — was a serious student of literature. His
library stretches across worlds and civilizations. His
reading ventures span most fields of human knowledge,
with special emphasis on religion, philosophy, and the
arts, in that order.

Dan Cameron was a religious man. He often recalled as
a personal goal the report from Paul the apostle in his
letter to Timothy, "I have fought a good fight, I have

finished the course, I have kept faith." The selection of that apostolic statement was not mere rhetoric for Dan Cameron. Its precept was his life.

Van

There can scarcely be one farmer in Saskatchewan and few elsewhere in Canada whose farming has not been influenced in one way or another by Hadley Van Vliet, the long-time professor and head of the agricultural economics department at the University of Saskatchewan. Van died suddenly on December 8, 1968 and in the height of his career. He was only fifty-four.

His substantial influence through thirty years was three-fold: as a university teacher of economics, as a student of agricultural problems, and as an adviser to policy makers and to farmers themselves. He served all three with marked distinction and was to many the "Mr. Chips" of Saskatchewan agriculture. He died on the doorstep of his parents home in Quinton, the Saskatchewan town near which he had been born. And he died as he lived, without complaint and while helping someone else. He was helping to carry into the house a cherished piece of furniture bequeathed to his Dutch immigrant father and mother by his distinguished brother, Bill Van Vliet, who had been killed in a car accident only a few months before.

Hadley Van Vliet was many things to many people but to most who knew him he was known simply as "Van." Some did not even realize the "Van" was other than a given name. As a teacher he encountered many generations of students at the University of Saskatchewan. He started there in 1938 as an instructor in agricultural economics, became an assistant professor two years later, and in 1944 became professor and head of the department, a position he retained until his death.

His students were legion and together they are a large part of Canadian agriculture. Some went on to become cabinet ministers, others government administrators; some became directors of specialized governmental agencies at both the provincial and federal level; some became professors, some became farm leaders, some entered industry and business, and some returned to the farm. Most recall his influence upon them with affection and respect. Three of his students became Rhodes scholars and many others took awards of similar stature in Canada and abroad. Five were awarded the governor-general's medal as the most distinguished university graduate of the year. A large percentage of those attending his funeral in Saskatoon were former students.

As a scholar he travelled a path of distinction. He took the bachelor of science degree in agriculture from the University of Saskatchewan at the age of twenty, graduating with great distinction, and went on to take his master of science degree. For two years he studied agricultural economics at the University of Wisconsin, a school noted for its contribution to North American agriculture, but never got around to completing the thesis requirements for his doctoral degree.

While his contribution to scholarship is considerable, his scholarly works are few. He never wrote a book and could hardly bring himself to prepare a formal address or scholarly paper. He sometimes used to begin preparation of a paper for presentation to a meeting but the last page of the advance preparation nearly always concluded with "more to come." When his turn came to make the presentation few of the words which rushed out sounded at all like the original text. Frequently he spoke from scanty notes but usually he composed as he went along.

It was in the heat of actual debate that he really excelled. Sometimes this was at learned meetings of scholars, sometimes in conference rooms, but more often than not among groups of farmers. His style was unique. He could bend his lanky frame almost into knots and often discussed the most weighty of farm problems balanced on both knees atop anything that would hold his weight or with one foot atop, the other on the floor, and his chin resting on his uppermost knee. There must be countless tables around the country, in the rooms of both the meek and the mighty, which bear the imprint of his shoe.

Van was born on his father's farm near Quinton in the area which also gave birth to John James Deutsch, another distinguished scholar and public servant who at the time of his death was principal of Queen's University. It was often said by each of them that they shared a two-boy desk in a one-roomed country school house. While his desk mate travelled to many places and through many different spheres, Van remained in Saskatchewan but his influence travelled much the same road. It was the impact of the man's brilliant mind which impressed first, but it was his understanding and compassion which lingered.

He had almost total recall of just about anything he had ever read or experienced, and he tended to bring the whole bundle of experience to play on any subject. This was often confusing to students who expected more directness and clarity of expression than Van offered. But to others more mature, the depth and breadth of his understanding and knowledge were what mattered. He would often listen earnestly, reply "You betcha," then add a new dimension to the discussion by posing the question in a larger perspective. He spoke in a hurry as though there were not time enough to get it all out.

Van was honored in many ways. He was once president of the Saskatchewan Agricultural Graduates Association; he was president of the Saskatchewan Agricultural Economics Society; he was named a Fellow of the Agricultural Institute of Canada in 1968. But most of all he was honored by all who invited him to discuss and to debate agricultural policy issues.

Contentment

Del was a man who knew contentment. His parents had named him Winram Delbert Bryce Simes but most people he knew called him simply "Del." Some of his school chums had called him "The Doc." This may have been because his physician-father was "the doctor" in the town, and it may have been because he himself had thought of medicine as a career. But in later years that nickname was forgotten along with the medical career that never came to be. His mother and some of the older generation who were more proper always called him Delbert but for the rest it was always just "Del." In more than twenty years, which was the adult half of his life, I never recall anyone ever calling him "mister."

Del died in 1961 at the age of forty-one, and they buried him on the hillside above the valley near which he was born and overlooking the Saskatchewan town of Fort Qu'Appelle in which he lived most of his life. Aside from the informality and unpretentiousness of the man there are two other things which come to mind as having set his short life apart from many of his fellows. One was his contentment with the valley and the Fort as home and his apparent lack of desire to move elsewhere. He went away to college and occasionally on a business trip but he seemed quite satisfied to spend his years in one place. He even acquired a cabin along one of the Qu'Appelle lakes for a summer place and spent his vacations not far from the Fort. The other was his close association with sickness and with the threat of death. It was almost as if he lived each day for itself never knowing really whether it might

not be his last. He was never very well, having contracted
diabetes at the age of five and at a time when therapy for
the disease was not so refined as it later became. It was the
thirty-six years of diabetes which damaged his kidneys and
took his life.

Del's father was "the doctor." Forty years earlier the
late Austin Bryce Simes was the country doctor at
Abernethy, just over the hills from the Qu'Appelle valley.
His mother had been a nurse. When Del was still a boy, his
father moved to the Fort to become the doctor to the
Indians who inhabit the Qu'Appelle reservations. When
the Indian Hospital was built at the Fort, Dr. Simes moved
into it as its chief, and Del grew up in a rambling house in
a cluster of trees not far from that hospital. When he
became a man, Del went to work at the hospital as its
pharmacist and after a few years as one of the druggists in
the Fort's only drug store.

Because the Fort is not a very big place, Del never lived
far from that hospital and many of his interests centered
around its work and its patients, the Indians of the
Qu'Appelle. Perhaps a lifetime of association with the
valley's original residents and their families, many still not
very sophisticated, brought Del to appreciate the simpler
things in life. I would think, however, it was more his
constant contact with sickness — in himself and others —
for the wants and needs of the sick are often quite simple.
They want release from pain, assurance of recovery, little
more.

I've often called at Del's place after a year or more of
moving from west to east and back again, and across the
seas and back to enquire "what's new" of him. The reply
was always the same: "Nothing much, you know. Everything's about the same." The truth of the matter was that
things were not always the same. He had married, and he
and Agnes had two sons. They had a new home. His father
had died. His sister married. He'd been to hospital again.
There'd been a fire. A new wing had been built onto the
old building and a new doctor had arrived. He had
another dog. One of the rose bushes had become poorly,

and he'd replaced it with a new type of plant. His mother had moved down east. A new car replaced the old. These are the kind of milestones which mark out any man's life, and they always change things as they come and go. The thing which was unchanged for Del was the man himself. He seemed to accept the joys and the sorrows as a part of the pattern of life, of his life.

I don't suppose he ever realized that his unchangedness was different from the norm, that most people were coming and going and he himself stayed. Some stay because they have to, and some because they want to. I don't suppose he realized there was a difference, and that his contentment was unusual in a world beset by dissatisfaction. I don't suppose he realized that there was a difference between making the best of adversity and making the most of life. It's idle now to speculate on his reasons. He took them with him when he died. But it is worthwhile to record that his constancy and contentment were noticed and were considered worth the notice.

Wheat Specialist Extraordinaire

Clive Davidson was raised on a homestead near Yellow Grass, Saskatchewan and devoted the rest of his life to the improvement of the grain industry in which the early settlers and their successors have tried to make a living for most of this century. He died in Winnipeg in 1974, at the age of seventy-two.

Many prairie farmers may not know about Mr. Davidson but they have certainly benefited in many ways from his work, and those who did meet him have been the better for that acquaintance. A close associate has said of him that "his humanity, wisdom, and capacity for friendship were matched only by a self-effacing attitude towards himself and his work."

Clive Davidson studied economics at the University of Saskatchewan, taking both the BA and MA degrees, and plunged into the grain industry at the outset of the depression. He joined the old Dominion Bureau of Statistics in 1930 as a grain statistician but was quickly seconded by the office of the prime minister, then the Right Honorable R. B. Bennett, as grain adviser. Mr. Davidson was assigned to help the late John McFarland bring a measure of stability to a chaotic Canadian wheat market at a time when markets everywhere were in turmoil, and he spent several years at that task. In 1933 he was sent as Canada's representative to the first meeting of the Wheat Advisory Committee in London which met after the failure of the first wheat agreement of 1933, and for the next thirty years he represented Canada at international meetings.

When the Canadian Wheat Board was established in 1935, Mr. Davidson became its first secretary but left after two years to establish an economic consulting firm of his own. On the outbreak of the Second World War he returned to the Wheat Board where he remained until his formal retirement in 1963, holding many senior positions: manager of the board's acreage department, statistician, secretary, and finally executive assistant to the board itself. He managed during his long career to undertake a number of special projects overseas relating to grain and agriculture in South America, the Middle East, and the Far East. After 1963 he joined an economic consulting firm in Winnipeg.

On many occasions he was involved in research projects sponsored by the Wheat Pools, and he remained throughout his life a vocal supporter of the farmers who tried to help themselves through the Wheat Pool associations. Not long before his death he prepared in collaboration with Dr. Merril Menzies, a lifetime colleague in the study of the Canadian grains industry, a special article carried in *The Western Producer* to mark the fiftieth anniversary of Saskatchewan Wheat Pool. Their message was simple: "not often do great dreams blossom into great realities."

Brock

His parents had named him John Hewgill Brockelbank, the first being a family name from his father's side and the second his mother's family name. Some friends called him plain "John," and he usually referred to himself as J. H. Brockelbank. But that's where the formality ended; for most of his eighty years nearly everyone else called him "Brock." Brock died May 30, 1977 in a Regina hospital after an automobile collision at a Regina intersection.

In his time he had lived many lives, the best known being his public life which included three decades of service to the Saskatchewan people as member of the legislature, cabinet minister, and senior statesman of Canada's original CCF party and later the NDP. I came to know his more private lives, and it is those I want to recall.

He was first a farmer's son, having been born on a farm in Grey County of Ontario on June 24, 1897. After some early schooling he came west with his parents who finally settled on three quarters of land near Rockhaven, around Wilkie in north-central Saskatchewan. Later he took to farming on his own account. After high school in Saskatoon he enlisted in what then was called Duval's draft of the 196th battalion and went overseas to join the Princess Patricia's Canadian Light Infantry with which he saw front-line service in France and Belgium. "The Pats" were one of Canada's most famous regiments of the First World War, and Brock always retained fond recollections of that wartime service, kept active membership in the Canadian Legion, and looked up former Pats buddies wherever he could find them.

Back home in 1919 he took steps like many others to find a farm of his own and wound up walking into the Bjorkdale area east of Saskatoon with a fellow veteran, to select acreage being offered by the Soldier Settlement Board. Bjorkdale became his home for many years. In 1920 his family urged him to take a short Normal school course being offered in Saskatoon so that he could become a teacher. The course started just after New Year's and was held in St. Thomas Presbyterian Church on Saskatoon's west side. After ten weeks he earned a temporary third-class teacher's certificate. By March he had acquired the school-teaching post at the Bjorkdale school just three miles from his homestead and on March 18 he opened his school room with four students. He eventually acquired a permanent third-class certificate.

Soon after he started teaching he met Peter Bell, another war-veteran homesteader who lived in the district with a brother, Tom, and his sister, Ellen, who kept house. In time Brock came to call more often at the Bell place and on January 20, 1921 he and Ellen Buchannan Bell were married.

Later in 1921 the Soldier Settlement Board told Brock he had to get on with his farming or they'd take away the homestead. In the spring of 1922 he gave up teaching, moved onto the land, and began farming in earnest. He once told me that at the time there were about nine acres under cultivation, and when the adjacent quarter became available he took it up. It had about twenty acres of fairly open land which he said he broke up right away. By the mid-1920s, he had forty to fifty acres in crop.

Brock stayed at farming through the 1930s and in 1938 ran for the legislature in the Tisdale riding surrounding his farm, as a candidate for the new CCF party which he had helped to organize. He and ten others were elected, the first socialists ever to be elected to a legislative body in North America. Later his constituency was renamed Kelsey. He was returned in six succeeding general elections and served for twenty-nine unbroken years until his voluntary retirement just before the 1967 general

election. He was a cabinet minister for twenty years and
served also as deputy premier. Only one or two others had
served for longer terms.

Others can speak with more authority on Brock's public
career. I knew him privately and I always considered him
a kind of private person. He remained throughout his life
very fond of family, his immediate family and more
distant kinfolk, and he was intensely loyal to friends. He
was one of the best visitors we ever had call at our place.
For years he used to drop into our Regina home for a brief
call on New Year's Eve and, after we moved to Saskatoon,
he often came around for an evening meal. In later years
he took to wine making in his home and was proud of his
output. He always brought a bottle for the table and
quickly learned that we preferred his mead, a white wine
made from honey, rather than the red of the chokecherry,
which seemed to be the more plentiful.

Many of his family are almost as well known across the
West as he was. He had three brothers and all survive,
living in retirement in British Columbia. E. E. (known as
Manley) lives in Victoria, Wilfrid C. in Kelowna, and
Clarence W. in Penticton. His widow survives him as do
three children. His son John followed him into the
Saskatchewan legislature in 1964, sitting for Saskatoon
Mayfair, and is Speaker of the legislature. Daughter Anna
married farmer Ted Skene who farms at Balcarres,
Saskatchewan, and Sally married Frank McCallion, a
teacher like Brock who came to work as a senior personnel
management officer for Saskatchewan Wheat Pool, the
farmer's co-operative Brock helped to organize in 1923
and joined in its first year. There are also seven grandchildren.

Relations

Memory Plays Strange Tricks

Memory sometimes plays strange tricks on the human consciousness. On Palm Sunday, for instance, some music and the sound of a group of men walking together down an aisle in church turned the clock back for me at least thirty years and brought forward a flood of memory from my boyhood. I was born into the Presbyterian persuasion whose practice in Canada is to observe the Lord's last supper with a communion service four times a year. The spring service usually falls at Easter time and sometimes on Palm Sunday. Many communion hymns are available and this time someone had selected an old favorite Scottish paraphrase whose words and music both came out of the eighteenth century. I recalled the opening lines as soon as the organ began its haunting melody:

'Twas on that night when doomed to know
The eager rage of every foe,
That night in which He was betrayed,
The Saviour of the world took bread. . . .

My mind recalled the double line of elders even before they came into my view as they walked slowly up the aisle to take their places in the front pews. My father had been part of that column every time I had taken communion in the old home church and indeed, when he died in 1969, had been a serving elder in that church for more years than any other. I must confess my eyes fogged over a bit as my mind recalled his slow walk to the front, in latter years almost a shuffle, as he worked his misshapen legs slowly and steadily forward to perform what he considered a most serious duty.

The communion table stood on a raised platform as it had in the old home church and was covered as before with a well-pressed white sheet. It had been the custom in the older church for two of the elders to raise the cloth gently, fold it carefully, and place it on a nearby pew. My father had been one of those two for all of the years I could remember, and the duty had become more difficult for him as the years passed because he found it less easy to stand. He knew as did the others that the elements laid beneath the cloth in their sparkling silver dishes and cups had been prepared the night before by his own hands. I recalled that he had performed that duty without missing a single time for most of the thirty years he served as an elder.

As the last of the elders took his place at the front and the minister stepped to the center, the congregation reached the final stanza of that old and haunting hymn:

With love to man this cup is fraught;
Let all partake the sacred draught;
Through latest ages let it pour,
In memory of My dying hour.

I had great difficulty bringing back my consciousness to the present which was meant to have significance by itself. It was the first communion for my wife and me as members of a new church in our new home in Saskatoon.* My memory kept pulling me back, and the faces before my slightly misty eyes were the faces of another time.

When we got home we had our usual after-church cup of coffee and quite by accident I picked up the latest copy of *The Presbyterian Record,* the magazine of Canada's Presbyterians. It chanced to fall open towards the back pages, and there to catch my eye was this historical note:

The congregation of First Presbyterian Church in Regina celebrated its fiftieth anniversary in January [1975]. . . . First Church may have been the first congregation formed by minority groups who did not

---

*St. Andrew's Presbyterian Church, Saskatoon, Saskatchewan

wish to become part of the United Church of Canada in 1925. The congregation was formed on 5th January 1925 immediately after it was known that all five former Presbyterian congregations in Regina had decided by majority vote to enter church union.

That was my home church, and my mother and father had been among its first members. Had Whitman Harold Phillips not died of complications arising from surgery intended to replace his worn-out hip joints, he would have marked his ninetieth birthday a few days after these words were written.

He had been born on a farm near Brougham village in Pickering township of Ontario. He came west in 1905 at the age of nineteen, first to work on a farm near Indian Head and later to farm with his father, the late Robert S. Phillips, near Regina city where they operated a market garden for years. For a time he was also a grain buyer at Pinkie station, four miles west of the city. Like many of his fellows he filed on a homestead (near Empress in northwest Saskatchewan) but returned to the city and took up the trade of carpentry. Later he established a building contracting business which he operated until his death.

Time Nor Tide Tarrieth No Man

I got to thinking about time the other day and especially about its limited supply when I came upon a comment by Charles William Eliot, one-time president of Harvard University in United States. He was quoted as saying to a newspaperman, "You have the worst job in the world. You never have time."

Most of us don't have as much time as we'd like. But my mother used to say to her three sons: you always have the time to do the things you want to do.

Henry Wadsworth Longfellow, the American poet who also became a college professor, wrote a number of memorable poems, among them "Hyperion," a romance which he wrote in 1839. His view of time was stated in the following words:

> Alas! It is not till Time, with reckless hand has torn out half the leaves from the Book of Human Life to light the fires of human passion with, from day to day, that man begins to see that the leaves which remain are few in number.

We've all heard the one about "time and tide waiting for no man." In recent reading I found what was likely the first expression of that idea by a man named Robert Greene, who wrote in the year 1592, "Time nor tide tarrieth no man."

A Presbyterian clergyman I have come to know* was asked not long ago to introduce me to a luncheon club as

---

*The Rev. R. A. Davidson, St. Andrew's Presbyterian Church, Saskatoon, Saskatchewan.

its invited speaker. During the introduction he told the story about a lady he used to visit in hospital where she was undergoing treatment for what came to be terminal cancer. He said she told him about a devotional radio program she had come to welcome during the long, tedious days in hospital bed, and she said to him, "You know, we don't take time to be holy." The minister said that taking part in a devotional was what that lady meant by being holy. He also said there now is a hymn in the new Book of Praise used in his church whose opening lines are these:

Take time to be holy
Speak oft with thy Lord.

He said he never hears that hymn without thinking on that patient lady who took time to be holy while her body was wasting away. Then he said that lady was my mother.

My mother was born Mary Elizabeth Wilson on a farm near Clayton, Ontario and died on October 30, 1951 as Mrs. Whitman Harold Phillips of cancer in a Regina hospital. She was sixty-six. As I often recall, she used to say there is always time to do what you want to do.

She came west to Qu'Appelle, Saskatchewan before the First World War to teach music and to conduct a church choir. After moving to Regina a few years later, she continued her music teaching until her marriage. An early temperance worker, she was for years an executive member of the Regina district and the Saskatchewan provincial WCTU. For years she was supervisor of Loyal Temperance Legion work in Regina's public schools and was instrumental in the introduction of temperance teaching in the Saskatchewan school curricula. She was also an executive member of the women's federation of her church and its women's missonary society.

Around the Old Piano

I stood around the piano the other night with a group of friends singing the old songs of not many years ago. You know the ones; they were the songs some of you sang like I did in the back of an army truck as it bounced along some dark road somewhere in western Europe or around a camp fire in the years since the end of the Second World War. Our children might think them rather tame, but my recollection is that some of them had words we didn't think ought to be aired in polite company.

The piano player was Shirley Phillips, my brother's wife, and she kept turning the pages of one song book after another, stopping to play any item someone wanted played, and the rest of us picked up the melody if not the words. Then she turned over the last of the books, and there, next to be played, was an old piece of sheet music that predated any war I knew anything about. It was a number out of the First World War and as Shirley began to play, the years tumbled away and I saw once again my own mother at the keyboard and heard her rich contralto voice coming back over the years. The next piece of sheet music and the rest of the stack had all belonged back in the years now gone. They had been well thumbed over and bore many marks of the passing years.

Consider, for example, this one. Anyone ever know, before the First World War, a song which began like this?

> Good-bye ma, good-bye pa,
> Good-bye mule with yer old hee-haw
> I may not know what this war's about
> But you bet by gosh I'll soon find out.

That was called "Long Boy" and those words were written by William Herschell in 1917, the year the United States came into that other war. The music was by Barclay Walker.

The next was an old favorite called "Casey Jones," which was the epic of the brave engineer who rode his train round a bend to his death. The music was written by Eddie Newton and the words by T. Lawrence Seibert back before that war, and they contained words of infidelity familiar to the world of today. Down about the third verse it went like this:

> Mrs. Jones sat on her bed asighing
> Just received word that Casey was dying
> Said go to bed children and hush your crying
> Cause you got another papa on the Salt Lake line.

There were some long-time favorites by song writers everyone now knows. Two items by Irving Berlin written back before the First World War were called "Call Me Up Some Rainy Afternoon" (1910) and "Ev'rybody's Doin' It Now" (1911). There were just stacks of the old music, sheet music of another era played many, many times on the piano for groups just like ours many years before. "Take Me Out to the Ball Game" came out in 1908 with words by Jack Norwood and music by Albert Von Tilzer. In 1912 it was "It's a Long Way to Tipperary" by Jack Judge and Harry Williams. In 1914 there was "When You Wore a Tulip, and I Wore a Big Red Rose" with words by Jack Mahoney and music by Paul Wenrich. George M. Cohan, one of the great masters of another time, wrote "Over There" in 1917, the song which had the American doughboys marching through the cities of Europe.

It was indeed a nostalgic evening for many of us around that piano. The music had been bought originally by Mary Elizabeth Wilson, some of it back in Lanark county of Ontario and some of it in Saskatchewan after Miss Wilson came west to play the organ in the Anglican church in the town of old Qu'Appelle. That's what she always called it to distinguish the main-line town from the fort which bore the same name.

In the east she had called herself Mayme Wilson but the sheet music bought after she came west was marked in her own hand with Mamie Wilson, the spelling by which we always knew her. Years later Miss Wilson came to Regina, married Whitman Harold Phillips, and they raised three sons. Many times the whole family and others who came to visit have stood around the piano singing those same old songs and, as I recall it, every time one or other of the old songs brought a tear to my eye.

The other night was no exception. It was only a few days after Remembrance Day and I had many memories of that war. My brother Wilson who enjoys singing around a piano was there and, every time a particular favorite came up, he would nudge me with his elbow and be the first to try the melody. And the songs themselves. There were others in the room, some of them old enough to remember those old songs when they were young and the songs were new. It was altogether a wonderful evening of remembrance.

The Old Homestead

Some editors have the good fortune to have been born on a farm; others have to settle for an early life in some city and the prospect of marrying a farmer's daughter. I was one of the latter and married into the family of a farmer who with his brother had pioneered a settlement in northern Saskatchewan. Recently I accompanied my wife and her sister back to the homestead; one had returned on occasion before, but for the other it was the first visit in twenty-five years.

It was an interesting experience and one I am sure must have been shared by many men who have been taken back home to visit their wife's childhood haunts. This is what I learned from our return visit:

• The village had got a lot smaller, especially the main street which had shrunk more than anyone would expect.

• The general store wasn't nearly as imposing as it used to be.

• Even the beer parlor had changed, or at least so the visitors suspected, because now it had become a mixed beverage room, and they were permitted inside for the first time. Many of its afternoon sippers were former school chums and the reunions could have lasted all day.

• The river on the way to the home farm had become less turbulent and wasn't even as wide as it used to be. In fact, it would be difficult to understand now how anyone might have got stuck in trying to ford it with a loaded wagon.

• The road leading to the home place had been allowed

to run to ruts and hollows without any gravel like it used to have. In the rainy season, the time we chose for our visit, it couldn't even be navigated all the way to the farmhouse.

• The house itself needed paint although some improvement was evident: the new owner had installed the power line and there was a yard light for the first time. But how much improvement that really meant was haughtily debated because the sisters recalled that in their time there were lights in every room too, lights provided by the battery system installed by their innovative father.

• The old outhouse was gone but the woodpile where it used to be remained and the small tree planted nearby by mother had weathered the intervening years and now was one of the healthiest trees on the place. It was a black poplar too.

• The road leading down to the pasture remained but it had become overgrown in many places because there weren't cows anymore.

It was a nostalgic return, the kind everyone should either have or witness at least once in a lifetime. How many of you have been back to the old home place in the last twenty-five years?

Centenary Celebration

One of my sons asked why I had picked 1976 to visit Virginia and I said the reason was because it was the two hundredth anniversary of the United States' Declaration of Independence. His response was that I shouldn't forget that 1976 was also the hundred and ninth anniversary of the Canadian Confederation and that got me to thinking about my father's flag pole.

It was early in the year 1967 that a delivery van pulled up to the family home in Regina and the man headed to the front door with one end of a package that extended almost all the way from his truck at the street. When the door was answered he said, "That will be $85.62 collect please," and got something less than an enthusiastic response from a family member who wanted to know, "What's in that funny looking package?" Turned out it was my father's new flag pole, ordered from the factory collect without anyone else having been told about it.

As I recall it, that was a cold spring and it wasn't until late June that we finally got around to thinking about how to put up father's flag pole at Lumsden Beach, site of the family cottage for many years. He got a bit more uneasy as June slipped away and kept saying he wanted his flag pole in place for July first so that he could fly Canada's new maple-leaf flag on the country's hundredth birthday along with the blue-and-white centennial flag.

My brother and I finally got down to the installation job on the morning of July 1 itself and working against great odds got it installed in time to raise the flags before sundown. The odds were the incessant prodding from father who knew all about installing flag poles although I don't recall he had ever done one before, and the dreariness of the weather. My recollection was that it rained most of the morning and before we got the job finished a few snowflakes had fallen too. That's how I shall always remember Canada's one hundredth birthday: the flag pole, the new Canadian flag, father excitedly grinning as the flags gave their first snap in the stiff breeze. And, of course, the rain and the snow on July 1.

Screevers

I had my first "screever" the night I met Lilian Gibb. It was at her home in the Kerrisdale district of Vancouver and the occasion followed the rehearsal for my own wedding to occur the following day. I met her at the door, a spacious door I came to know well in later years, and her welcome made me feel at once that I'd come back.

"So, you are Bub," she said with her thick Scottish tongue. "I've heard a great deal about you, laddie."

My response was in the same lighthearted mood: "And I've heard about you too. Do you mind if I call you Aunt Lil?"

That all happened more than twenty-five years ago, and I learned through the years that most who had ever heard of this amazing lady did in fact call her "Aunt Lil" although some preferred to call her "Gibbie." The last time I saw Aunt Lil was in late 1976 in Victoria when members of her family gathered to help honor her ninety-sixth birthday. She was still quite fit. She stepped out with us for a dinner in a fine hotel and even helped to toast her future. Soon after that party Aunt Lil developed some disturbing symptoms and after Christmas was taken to hospital for some tests. These led to surgery and the doctors found it was simply too late for effective therapy. She died quietly on January 16, 1977 of cancer, aged ninety-six years and nearly half a century after she had moved to Vancouver from Saskatoon because the coastal elevation and climate would be good for her declining health.

Lilian Gibb was born in Scotland, on September 23,

1880, the eighth of ten children born to Thomas Smith and his wife Amelié Liddiard, an Englishwoman. Mr. Smith was a farmer as had been the men of his family for generations and farmed property known as the Mains of Fowlis not far from Dundee in Perth county. My wife's paternal grandmother had also been a Smith, a sister to Lilian, and that is how this lady got to be known as "Aunt Lil" in my connection. Many others simply came to use the name.

Lilian Smith was married to Alexander Macdougal Gibb, a Scottish businessman, on February 1, 1908 and they came to Canada together a few months later and settled in Saskatoon. Mr. Gibb, known in the connection as "Uncle Sandy" and to his wife as "Snookies," died in Vancouver in 1947.

In both Saskatoon and Vancouver her church became her life. Lilian and Sandy Gibb became charter members of St. Thomas Presbyterian Church and Mr. Gibb was a member of its first board of managers. Mrs. Gibb helped to organize a CGIT unit at St. Thomas, the first in Saskatoon, and later headed a women's guild to help furnish the new St. Andrews theological college on the University of Saskatchewan campus.

She had a fine contralto voice and competed in music festivals, often taking a medal for solo performance. For years she was in demand as a soloist at church and for Robbie Burns nights and fowl suppers in the country-side.

I don't know when Aunt Lil made her first screever or how they got to have that name. But over the years she must have made several million of them. During the generation she lived in Saskatoon they became her trademark, screevers and her work for the church. Her home was always open to young people and most of the student ministers who came to St. Andrews found their way to it. I've met several of them who became ministers and everyone knows about her screevers.

To the uninitiated a screever is really a little pancake, something a bit larger than a silver dollar. Aunt Lil served them cold, sometimes with butter or jam. Many over the years have tried to duplicate Aunt Lil's screevers but none has matched her skill. My wife Tanyss dug out Aunt Lil's recipe, dictated by Aunt Lil; she herself never used a recipe. This is what she said must be done:

A squeeze of lemon, five "niffies" (what Aunt Lil called a handful) of flour, half a teaspoon of cooking salt, a pint of buttermilk, and a teaspoon of soda. Mix one big egg into a large niffie of brown sugar before adding the buttermilk. Then add the rest. Lather the griddle with butter or fat and cook for three minutes on each side. In later years she was given an electric frypan which she used instead of the griddle, setting it at 350 degrees.

When she moved to Vancouver her church work continued much as it had in Saskatoon — the church was Knox United — and her home again became a center mainly for young people. One of her main activities with young people was her junior choir. She called the youngsters "my bairns" and for them she always had a supply of little pancakes and jam — she found that youngsters could not easily say the strange word screever.

Aunt Lil was not a fussy housekeeper, nor was she a meticulous gardener. Her favorite place in the garden was called "hell's corner," a spot farthest from the house in the shade of some large trees. I did not go to Vancouver for the funeral but a niece who did said she visited hell's corner on the afternoon Aunt Lil died and a strange thing happened. She said the birds of every description descended on the corner, perched on every tree and post available, and just sat there silently as though they were offering a quiet requiem. It had brought a tear to her eye. Then the birds all left and none returned for about a week.

Always Helping Others

"She did many things for many people all through her life. That's why there were so many in the church. We all liked Mrs. Kanuka." That comment and others were made one day in 1967 as we drove slowly behind the hearse that bore the frail body of a kind and gentle lady, Anne Kybida Kanuka, to her final resting place on the outskirts of the city of Regina that had been her home in the new world for more than a third of Canada's first century. Her story may not differ greatly from that of many others who sought the promise and opportunity of a young Canada, away from the aged and hard trials of the old world. But her story I have come to know and I believe it worth retelling as one example of the struggle which brought Canada to its centenary.

We had just left St. Basil's Greek Catholic Church on Toronto Street, a church Mrs. Kanuka and her husband John and her family and many friends had helped to build. Her husband was among the founding members of the parish in the years before 1930 and both together had helped in more recent years to build the new church which had been dedicated only seven years. Some who joined sadly in the final rites of that strange, colorful, and enchanting Ukrainian service had been in St. Basil's parish before Mrs. Kanuka arrived from eastern Poland one day in 1930. Some had been born within the parish since her arrival, among them children and grandchildren of her own family. Together the generations and the two worlds mixed, each in its own way paying tribute to a friend who did many things for many people all through her life.

It had not been a long life — only three score and ten —
but in many ways it had been a very satisfying one. Mrs.
Kanuka was only thirty when her husband left her with
their first child in southeastern Poland to seek by himself a
new life in the new world. He came to western Canada and
after a time settled in Regina with a job on the railway.
Four years later Mrs. Kanuka and their son joined him
and together they lived in St. Basil's parish for nearly
thirty-seven years.

After the burial the family and friends returned to the
parish hall of St. Basil's for lunch. It was there her elder
son Fred spoke, first uncertainly in Ukrainian and then
confidently in English, of his mother's love for her church
and her friends in St. Basil's parish around which her
whole life revolved. Her family have all left the parish
now. Fred had become a teacher in Calgary, another a
lawyer in Regina, and her daughter, after training as a
nurse, married and raised a family in Regina. Together
they have fourteen children.

Three of John Kanuka's friends came back to join him,
bringing with them all the memories of the unfolding
years. The four men had come to Canada together nearly
forty years before and through the years had seldom met.
Now, on the death of Mrs. Kanuka, they returned, one
from Edmonton, one from Toronto, and one from
Thunder Bay.

But the story of her death and funeral is not one of
remembrance only. It can also be considered symbolic of
the change in the times of once lonely people who had
great troubles in coming to make a home in the new world.
Regina was my home town and I know only from travel
about the loneliness of a strange place. Regina must have
been more than strange, for it was for many of Mrs.
Kanuka's thirty-five years here also a cold and cruel place.
Mrs. Kanuka knew the worst of the trying times of the
depression, for her start here came at the beginning of the
1930s, when jobs were scarce.

In the years since, times have changed. There has been a
mixing of the traditional with the new. At the funeral the

somber head shawls of the older people blended with the fashionable hats of their children: the young college graduates and the professionals and the new world businessmen sat shoulder to shoulder with the older people who had been mainly hewers of wood and drawers of water for their more modest living. The service was in Ukrainian and English so that both generations could share in the warm words spoken in tribute to Mrs. Anne Kybida Kanuka.

Her driving force had propelled two sons and one daughter through the English-language schools and colleges of the new world until each was able to claim a professional career equal to any whose parents had started here. Her kindly persistence had also helped to build the new church where friends from the homeland could worship as their families had worshipped through many centuries and where she could do many things for many people, as her lifelong friends have said in tribute. Her living had helped many to bridge the gap between the old world and the new.

It is lives like hers, doing many things for many people, quietly encouraging youngsters and finally thinking of others, that made Canada a better place during its first 100 years and gives new promise for years yet to come in the second century.

Gentle Soul from Scotland

She had been born in Glasgow along the banks of the Clyde, not far from where the gentle hills meet the spray of the sea. In another land far from the sea, she was laid to rest in a prairie grave in the gently rolling countryside near where the Pipestone Creek meets the old Scottish settlement of Moosomin, Saskatchewan. Ann Penelope Mac-Pherson died as she had lived, gently, quietly, and among her loving family and friends. At her death in 1967, she was nearly eighty-two.

From her Scottish homeland she had come, as did many others, as a First World War bride. She had married John Archie MacPherson who was of settlers' stock. His family homesteaded along the Pipestone the year after the railway reached Moosomin, then the capital city of old Assiniboia on the northwest frontier.

Her funeral in Moosomin's St. Andrew's Presbyterian Church was something like the gathering of the clans. There were, of course, some MacPhersons — the surviving brothers and sisters of her deceased husband, their families, and her family. There were also MacDonalds, MacDougalls, MacKenzies, and Stewarts. And there were the others, also sons and daughters of the pioneers — the Allisons, the Broughs, the Deans, the Drummonds, the Jamiesons, and the Morrows; the McEwens, the Phins, the Sinclairs, the Tanners, and the Waltons.

There were two ministers — one from St. Andrew's which had been her church and the other from Regina's First Presbyterian Church where her younger daughter was a choir member. It was a soft and gentle service with

the music from the choir and congregation rolling like the
gentle slopes which amble from the glens to the Clyde in
the homeland. The newer generation of girls joined by one
man had come back to St. Andrew's choir for the funeral
to honor their old friend. The first of two hymns was a
favorite from the Scottish Psalter:

> I to the hills will lift mine eyes;
> From whence doth come mine aid,
> My safety cometh from the Lord,
> Who heaven and earth hath made.

There was a reading from "the guid book," the prayers,
and then a gentle, quiet word from the young minister
from Regina who, although he had known Mrs. MacPherson only briefly in her final weeks, said he had come to
consider her a kindred spirit. Then came the final hymn,
the Scottish paraphrase which for generations has com-
forted and strengthened Scots in their wanderings:

> O God of Bethel by Whose hand
> Thy people still are fed;
> Who through this weary pilgrimage
> Hast all our fathers led. . . .

Out into the dazzling March sunshine and the frosty air
the six young friends bore the casket with the body of Ann
Penelope MacPherson, past an honor guard of six older
friends who had been with her in the Ladies' Auxiliary to
Moosomin's Canadian Legion, a group of which Mrs.
MacPherson had been a charter member.

Although she had been one among many Scots to settle
both before and since "the war" along the CPR main line
which runs through Moosomin to the Pacific, she was set
apart from many by her gentleness of spirit. She was in the
beginning an educated lady, having attended the University of Glasgow where she attained her master of arts
degree, a distinction of which she was justly proud. She
became a teacher at home and even after coming to
Canada for a time. She had met John Archie MacPherson
when he was on leave during the First World War. They
were married before it was over, and she followed him to

Canada in 1920 to make a new home away from home. After a number of teacherages, they settled in Moosomin where Mr. MacPherson became the school principal. In later years he gave up teaching for the public service.

When he died Mrs. MacPherson moved to Regina with her younger daughter Joanne, who was a deputy registrar of land titles. The elder daughter Marion, a senior foreign-affairs officer with Canada's external affairs department, was at the time a staff member with Canada's permanent mission to the United Nations and later became High Commissioner to Sri Lanka. Their only son, William, whom Mrs. MacPherson always called Billy, was then managing editor of the *Ottawa Citizen*. Bill and his wife, the former Bev Wright also of Moosomin, have four children, the only MacPherson grandchildren — Colin, Seonag, Lachlan, and Morag.

Anyone who came to know Mrs. MacPherson would know she was beyond all else a gentle soul. Gentle in most matters anyway and with only a few exceptions. One was her church and another her politics. And then there was Scotland about which the friendly jest was allowed only on occasion. She used to chuckle when told of another friend whose father considered himself fortunate to have been born a Scot, a Presbyterian, and a Liberal, which he said were "three wondrous works of the Lord." Mrs. MacPherson firmly agreed on all three.

Finally, Retirement

There's a story out on Vancouver Island that when spring comes, the natives who have a place to sell dust off the "for sale" sign, fix up their rose bushes so the blossoms will be seen easily from the roads and just sit back and wait for "the suckers from Saskatchewan." My mother-in-law attests to that story. She says she heard it first in a conversation between two natives riding ahead of her on a local bus. Besides, my mother-in-law also comes from Saskatchewan.

My favorite Vancouver Island location was on the outskirts of the city of Courtenay called Mission Hill. It was so named long ago, they say, because this land was once deeded to the Church of England to support its work in the new world. The church built its first mission in this part of the island near this spot and later sold much of the land to support church expansion elsewhere. A small Anglican church still stands near the bottom of the hill at a spot not far from the original mission.

Up here on the hill nearly everyone comes from "back east," which to the native British Columbian means from the other side of the mountains. Many of them call Saskatchewan their home. Before coming this way, many to live in retirement, they operated railways, farmed wheat, kept stores, were stenographers and school teachers. Out here they're not really native but they're not strangers either. The prairie people have brought a new breeziness to the island and, of course, they've absorbed something of the island into their own features, changing them too.

Looking out from the window where I sit for breakfast, you can see Comox Bay and the blue waters of the Pacific. On a clear day you can also see the mountains of the mainland beyond. Behind our house are the pines and firs of the British Columbia timberline and just to the west of the hill is a fertile valley with more mountains beyond that again. It's difficult to live in this setting even for a month without absorbing something of the maritime complexion. One can even smell the kelp from the sea.

People who retire out here usually buy enough land to keep a big garden — enough room for all the flower color they want and plenty besides for the vegetable patch. Gardening is the hill's main diversion and I dare say the main occupation of most islanders over sixty years of age and still able.

I have yet to meet a man of any age on Vancouver Island who does not own a fishing rod. Most own several. Whenever they can, they're out flicking flies into the rustling trout streams that swish down from the mountains to join the sea right at everyone's own back door, or they are out on the chuck itself trying to wrestle in a salmon for dinner.

People on this part of the island, especially those from "back east," like to go on picnics. It's usually an all-day outing. The menfolk head up stream as soon as the picnic site is located for an hour or so of fly casting. When they get hungry (or when they catch enough trout to go around) they head back, and dinner (often beans and bacon) is cooked on an open fire beneath the tall timber. The island is loaded with government-operated camping grounds, all of them with running water, fireplaces, and wood supplied, and many with tenting facilities.

Contrasts of living conditions are marked on Vancouver Island, more marked than people over the mountains would ever guess. In Victoria and in a few other old and sedately settled towns, life is slow, orderly, and unruffled like it was for many in the old land of England. Some say that Victoria with its flower pots along the main streets and its old, moustached gentlemen with cane and umbrella

looking for crumpets with their tea is more English than
England. Conditions are quite different "up island," as
goes the expression for describing country north of the city
of Victoria. Up island is rugged and rough. It is, in many
sections, real frontier country with as few conveniences as
you find on many a backwoods farm on the northern
fringe of the prairies.

My guess is that it's not entirely the roses which attract
exiles from Saskatchewan. Many are looking, of course,
for an "easier" climate where life is not so hard on them
physically. Many more, however, are really looking for a
new frontier (perhaps one not quite so rugged). There is
still a wild, virginal quality to the Vancouver Island
mountains, to the streams that flow down from them, and
to the roads and the fields that nestle at their feet. It is this,
I think, which helps to attract and hold the man and
woman from Saskatchewan, many of whom broke new
prairie land to the plough and came to love and to want
something unspoiled, unsophisticated, something virginal
about their surrounding. They have found that up island.
With their neighbors who sought the same goals, they have
found new friends and have built themselves a good community.

Index

Bob Phillips was born in Regina and went through its school system, including a year at Regina College which then offered first-year university. In 1941 he joined the Canadian army and served overseas. Later he took an honors degree in economics and political science at the University of Saskatchewan in Saskatoon and began the first of two careers.

In 1948 he became a newspaperman, a trade which took him to Vancouver, Windsor, Ont., Toronto, back to Regina, overseas again to London and to Toronto again. During the next twelve years he worked as reporter, deskman, editorial writer, city editor, wire-service staff writer and editor for *The Canadian Press; The Leader-Post,* his hometown paper in Regina; *United Press* in Europe and *The Canadian Press* again.

In 1960 he began a second career as a professional economist and became research analyst for Saskatchewan Wheat Pool, the first they had employed, and in time established the Pool's research division and became its first director. In 1973 he combined the two careers to become editor and publisher of *The Western Producer,* a weekly newspaper for farmers which has been owned by the Wheat Pool since 1931.

He now lives in Saskatoon with his wife Tanyss, an economist and a westerner. Their two sons (Sandy born in London and Peter in Toronto) have come to call the West home and are learning about the joys of being away and coming back again.